Public/Private

Public/Private

Paul Fairfield

ROWMAN & LITTLEFIELD PUBLISHERS, INC.
Lanham • Boulder • New York • Toronto • Oxford

ROWMAN & LITTLEFIELD PUBLISHERS, INC.

Published in the United States of America
by Rowman & Littlefield Publishers, Inc.
A wholly owned subsidiary of The Rowman & Littlefield Publishing Group, Inc.
4501 Forbes Boulevard, Suite 200, Lanham, Maryland 20706
www.rowmanlittlefield.com

PO Box 317
Oxford
OX2 9RU, UK

British Library Cataloguing in Publication Information Available

Library of Congress Cataloging-in-Publication Data

Fairfield, Paul, 1966-
Public/private / Paul Fairfield.
p. cm.
Includes index.
ISBN 0-7425-4957-7 (cloth : alk. paper) — ISBN 0-7425-4958-5 (pbk. : alk. paper)
1. Privacy, Right of. I. Title.

JC596.F35 2005
323.44'8—dc22 2005016648

Printed in the United States of America

∞™ The paper used in this publication meets the minimum requirements of American National Standard for Information Sciences—Permanence of Paper for Printed Library Materials, ANSI/NISO Z39.48-1992.

Contents

Chapter One

Negotiating a Distinction

The categories public and private have long been fundamental to liberal-democratic understandings of social life. Political and moral ills are not remedied by means of state action without first considering whether such ills lie within the public domain, an essential precondition of institutional measures carrying the force of law. Yet however elementary the distinction between public and private may be in modern constitutional democracies, it is a distinction that invites confusion and ambivalence with respect to both its abstract meaning and its practical applications. Advocates of a right to privacy increasingly cite this troubled distinction, even as critics of the distinction question its conceptual coherence and the implications of its traditional interpretation.

In the present age of science-technology and the dawning age of information, the impression is growing that privacy is under threat in ways wholly unlike those of former times. The proliferation of information technology, information commerce, databanks trading information about persons without their knowledge or consent, and increasing preoccupations with security make possible both violations of privacy and other potentially ominous forms of social control. Coupled with this phenomenon is a widespread inclination among public authorities to involve themselves ever more in the personal affairs of individuals. While typically benign in intention, public institutions appear increasingly willing to restrict or override judgments hitherto private in the interests of utility, both individual and collective.[1] Within the general culture as well, intrusions into private life are everyday phenomena. Modern societies have become increasingly urbanized, overcrowded, and oddly fascinated by exposure, an appetite nourished by media and surveillance practices to which we have become accustomed.

Under these conditions the sphere of private life may need to reassert itself—and reassert itself it has within certain areas of public policy. Yet efforts to this end are beset with difficulties of several kinds, not least of which are the ways in which the private sphere has for centuries been understood (and misunderstood), the injustices to which its misunderstandings have long given rise, and the general difficulty in negotiating the distinction between public and private life. No little confusion surrounds the question concerning which domains of decision making rightfully fall within the jurisdiction of public rule and which belong to individuals as private agents. The confusion is nourished by issues that may be claimed with some legitimacy to be simultaneously public and private and by hybrid institutions that appear neither altogether one nor the other. Whether a private corporation contracted to deliver a public service is an essentially private or public matter is as far from being self-evident as whether aborting a pregnancy, engaging in unconventional sexual practices, or consuming narcotics falls under the category of public or private acts. There is room for doubt whether a general answer may be found to the question of the conditions under which a decision affecting an individual's life rightfully belongs to the individual and when it belongs to the majority of citizens.

Those who would navigate the distinction between public and private, accordingly, are faced with several daunting questions. First, is the distinction conceptually intelligible? Second, if it is, how is the distinction drawn? Third, what is the proper relation between the public and private spheres? Finally, what are the implications for public policy of a right to privacy should a reasonable basis be found for such a right? While these are logically distinct questions, answering them will require having recourse to a common line of argument relating to some fundamental issues of social life. In light of the intimate interconnection of the issues before us, it is unlikely that any will be satisfactorily resolved in isolation from the rest.

To orient matters, it will be useful to recall briefly how and why theorists both ancient and modern drew this fundamental distinction in political philosophy. It was the Greeks who first separated the domains of public and private, a distinction that they elevated (somewhat characteristically) into a dichotomy. The private realm was conceived as the household (*oikos*), wherein family life naturally resided. It was the domain in which familial ties were fostered; in which processes of reproduction, birth, and death took place; and where activities concerning the natural necessities of life were carried out. It included matters of economics and material sustenance, which belonged as well to the realm of necessity, which the Greeks contrasted with the sphere of human freedom. The household was also the appointed realm of the feminine, of women engaged in affairs of domestic life to which nature had ostensibly commissioned them.

In contrast, the public sphere (*polis*) was the domain of free (male) citizens coming together on an equal basis to resolve issues of state. Whereas the household was the site of inequality and natural necessity, public life constituted a nobler sphere which called upon such characteristically human capacities as reason, freedom, and civic virtue. For the Greeks, the primacy of politics had its foundation in a philosophy of human nature for which particular traits and capacities are hierarchically ordered. Since it was reason that constituted the distinguishing characteristic of human life—that which elevated the species categorically above the subhuman order—and since it was in the public realm that this capacity was principally exercised, public life assumed a quality of nobility denied to the private sphere. As Jean Bethke Elshtain observes, "the private person or *idiot* was a being of lower purpose, goodness, rationality, and worth than the *polites* or public citizen who belonged to and participated in the city."[2] The primacy of political over domestic life, then, reflected the metaphysical primacy of reason and freedom over the realm of necessity which human beings shared with the lower animals. It reflected as well the hierarchies of male over female, adult over child, and free citizen over slave. In the *Republic*, Plato went so far as to eliminate the private sphere altogether on the premise that it sows seeds of division within the city by elevating particularist, personal ties over public ends. Plato's famous proposal that wives, children, and property be held in common is a well-known case in point. While for his part Aristotle, with characteristic good sense, would not recommend measures as extreme, the *Politics* nevertheless perpetuated the dichotomous and hierarchical arrangement of public and private. Public life was the site of authority, reason, and the virtues of civic involvement. Citizens, while a minority of persons, were equal participants in a common endeavor to live the good life. Domestic life was a necessary complement and precondition of public life, yet it was a decidedly subaltern realm of passion over reason, particularity over universality, and necessity over freedom. Man, most ultimately, was a political animal, and while he was simultaneously a being within nature and the family—therefore within the household—it was in the realm of public affairs alone that he realized his essential humanity.

The denigration of the private sphere was axiomatic to Greek conceptions of politics and human affairs generally. It was a logically inescapable consequence of ethical and metaphysical doctrines fundamental to Greek thought concerning such matters as relations between the sexes, the nature of the good life, and the distinguishing attributes of human existence. Several such assumptions survived into the modern era, informing once again efforts of political thinkers to identify the proper relation between public and private life. Yet the distinction also took on new meaning and importance in the modern age, as classical liberals sought to found politics directly upon philosophies of the individual. For liberals of the early modern period, the private sphere bears less upon family life than upon the individual. The separation of public and private spheres serves essentially to distinguish areas of decision making that rightfully belong to political institutions from those belonging to persons as private agents. Early liberals worried in ways that their forebears had not about the public domain overwhelming the individual or intruding into the private affairs of citizens. Since persons by nature were free, rational, and equal, they were ill served by public institutions that reduced them to the status of subjects.

For classical liberals, the private sphere continues to include the household, wherein in accordance with tradition the husband and father is assumed to preside. The combined weight of custom and natural law had deemed that women, children, and domestic servants assume subordinate positions within the household, as feminists and other social critics would later decry. Yet the private sphere would also incorporate economic life, including not only matters of domestic economy but market relations broadly conceived. Liberals of this era are inclined to regard property as not only that belonging to the private domain but as itself a fundamental category of political thought. John Locke is an obvious case in point, whose *Two Treatises of Government* proffers a view of the social contract as effecting a state whose primary purpose is to safeguard what are essentially private ends—life, liberty, and property. Public institutions are fashioned to ensure private purposes no less, and perhaps more essentially, than communal ends. Accordingly, the private sphere in modernity would lose its Greek connotation as a lesser realm of affairs, instead assuming a stature and normative importance that it had previously lacked. The acquisition of wealth and property belongs no longer to the order of necessity but to the higher order of human freedom and virtue.

Intermediate in the classical liberal scheme of things between the household and the state is the realm of civil society. Voluntary associations such as corporations, clubs, churches, professional organizations, and so on are neither public nor private in the narrow sense of these terms but occupy a middle position sometimes termed "the social."[3] More often, however, liberals incorporate civil society into the private sphere to distinguish it clearly from the realm of the political—that is, the state. Business firms and property in particular are described as private in order to protect the marketplace from excessive political intervention. Economic life is an affair of individuals pursuing private ends through the free exchange of goods and services, just as other voluntary associations that are intermediate between the individual and the state engage persons in practices of civic—not political—involvement. While some liberals would prefer to speak of civil society as belonging to the public realm, thus distinguishing it from the private sphere conceived narrowly as the household,[4] the more common view is to conceive the public domain as the domain of government and the private sphere as the realm of individuality, the household, the marketplace, and civil society in general.

The elevation in status, then, of the private in modern times coincides with a broadening of its interpretation. The private sphere would be the site not only of personal undertakings and family life but of civic participation in its myriad forms. As a philosophy profoundly committed to human freedom, one of liberalism's principal concerns would be to safeguard private life from undue intrusion by public institutions in both its older, absolutist forms as well as its contemporary forms—state-sponsored paternalism, for instance, or unlimited majoritarianism. One of liberalism's most celebrated causes, in both its classical and its contemporary manifestation, is to defend individual judgment and conscience against aggressive majorities and the state apparatus at its command.[5] Public institutions and public opinion alike are typically viewed with a measure of suspicion, even as in other respects the public sphere continues to be conceived in modernity largely as it had been for the Greeks—as the domain of sovereign authority, rationality, freedom, and civil association.

More recent times have witnessed an emerging preoccupation with the value of privacy, a narrower realm of concern than that which occupied classical liberals, albeit one directly related to and entailed by traditional liberal concerns. James Fitzjames Stephen, Samuel Warren, and Louis Brandeis, writing in the latter nineteenth century, began to speak of a right of privacy as a method of protection against such emerging realities as an intrusive press and technological advances that made it increasingly possible to trespass upon "the sacred precincts of private and domestic life."[6] As Stephen writes,

> Legislation and public opinion ought in all cases whatever scrupulously to respect privacy. . . . All the more intimate and delicate relations of life are of such a nature that to submit them to unsympathetic observation, or to observation which is sympathetic in the wrong way, inflicts great pain, and may inflict lasting moral injury.[7]

Warren and Brandeis's influential article of 1890 argued in defense of an individual right of privacy particularly in light of a press that had become increasingly disposed to overstep traditional bounds of propriety by publishing intimate and damaging information about newsworthy individuals. Contemporary interest in privacy has arisen not only within scholarly circles but equally within the general population as perceptions that privacy is under threat appear increasingly justified.

Yet efforts to enhance or restore the sphere of private life, as mentioned, have met with major challenges. Among these is a powerful critique from feminists, who lament the traditional liberal-democratic habit of conceiving of the public and private spheres as being sharply opposed. The public/private dichotomy, these scholars argue, is among the political doctrines of the past that have served for generations to rationalize gender inequality, domestic violence, and other forms of injustice. Feminist literature has documented the myriad ways in which appeals to privacy have shielded forms of domination upon which political institutions are incumbent to prevent and remedy. This critique of the public/private dichotomy, as I argue in what follows, is compelling. Yet the persuasiveness of the critique does not bring the matter to an end. Instead, it raises new sets of questions regarding what, if any, scope remains for a private sphere, how to negotiate the shifting boundaries between public and private, or indeed whether notions of privacy and privacy rights retain any political and moral legitimacy in the wake of the feminist challenge. These are issues upon which feminist scholars disagree, as do liberal and other political philosophers who wish to concede the feminist critique without losing sight of the positive significance of privacy in the age of science-technology, information, and surveillance.

The issue, in short, is the standing of privacy as a political principle—its meaning, value, and relation to the public domain. The question of privacy is simultaneously a theoretical issue regarding a principle of justice and its possible justification as well as a practical question of its application within several areas of public policy. Identifying the scope and limits of privacy rights, or in general describing the proper relation between the public and the private in both abstract and concrete terms, is the challenge presented to students of politics by the feminist critique.

This chapter attempts to meet the theoretical challenge by examining the normative significance of privacy in social relations broadly conceived. After discussing feminist and other challenges to privacy in the following section, I advance the argument that privacy serves two fundamental purposes of equal importance in democratic societies. First, private life is the site in which individual autonomy, self-expression, and intimacy chiefly reside. A right of privacy protects persons both from other individuals and from aggressive majorities who may have little regard for individual inviolability. It provides public recognition to the fact that while citizens are members of a political body, they are also separate persons. The self is a contingent—even fragile—construction whose being and identity are not without political conditions of possibility, among which is a domain of privacy. The second role that privacy serves is to regulate social space in the interests of peace and civility. Privacy rights award legal form to tacit yet broadly shared understandings of the manner in which social relations are rendered civil by means of social and personal space. Privacy not only protects individuals against encroaching majorities, institutions, and technologies but plays a fundamentally civilizing role in our public involvements by regulating the moral distance between persons.

The following chapters turn to the practical question of applying privacy rights in several areas of public policy. Each takes up an issue in which privacy factors more or less prominently, examining theoretical arguments and legislative proposals reflecting the different sides of these debates. Since efforts to negotiate the public/private distinction are common to liberal-democratic societies, I investigate in these chapters a variety of legislative measures undertaken in different nations and jurisdictions rather than single out for discussion any one nation.

As Jean Cohen writes, "even if we acknowledge all the criticisms of the ideological versions of the public/private dichotomy, we still need the concepts of privacy and privacy rights."[8] The following studies concur fully with this view. While the point of view that they present may be described as liberal, they incorporate arguments advanced by many critics of liberalism, including, in particular, feminist critiques of traditional notions of public and private. Ancient philosophical dichotomies very often need to be transcended and none more so than the one before us.

THE PUBLIC/PRIVATE DICHOTOMY AND ITS CRITICS

It is commonplace for deep-seated moral or political convictions to assume the form of a grand either-or. Often, the stakes or passions involved seem to compel us either to assent to a given proposition or to oppose it with some vehemence, especially in today's increasingly polarized political climate. Refusal to do either, or efforts to find a third option, often seem like bad faith to the committed. Whether a choice that affects an individual's life rightly belongs to that individual or to the public at large is an example of this common phenomenon. One camp will urgently assert the right of a person to exercise his or her autonomy, that doing so is a private matter, a personal choice, or perhaps—as John Stuart Mill would say—a "self-regarding action."[9] With equal conviction, an opposing camp will assert that it is a public act, that the personal is political, and that, accordingly, all acts and choices belong in principle to the public domain. That it is one or the other is the premise of both camps. Fundamental normative distinctions, however, are often far less categorical in their meanings than what many of the committed would prefer, their interrelations and applications far more complex than how they may appear on first inspection or in abstract formulation. Negotiating the distinction between public and private is not a simple affair of carving up social reality into household and state, self-regarding and other-regarding action, or some other categorical polarity. It involves drawing distinctions in a manner that is hermeneutically informed by matters of both abstract principle and practical reality. It involves a capacity to see more than one side of an equation, to interpret moral contexts in more than one light, and to fashion judgments in a fallibilist spirit.

If the ancient Greeks and classical liberals were both inclined to regard the public and the private not only as a useful normative distinction but as a grand dichotomy, contemporary critics of both schools often proceed so far in the opposite direction that the distinction effectively disappears. Marxism, for instance, rejects the notion of a private sphere altogether as an ideological distortion. In a classless society, social affairs generally belong within the domain of politics. In particular, property is not to be held in private hands but belongs in principle to the public as a totality. Other socialists have taken positions ranging from the relatively strident and Marxist to more moderate views which, if not eliminating the private sphere, tip the scale decisively in favor of the public.

Recently, liberalism's communitarian critics have lamented the ways in which this doctrine has, in their view, given rise to a political culture of crass individualism. In the communitarian's estimation, calls for a right to privacy are symptomatic of the disintegration of community life which liberal individualism has brought about. Appeals to privacy are merely the latest move to privilege individual rights over communal and public ends. A better alternative, as one communitarian writes, is "to treat privacy as an individual right that is to be balanced with concerns for the common good—or as one good among others, without a priori privileging any of them."[10] This moderate proposal—barely, if at all, distinguishable from the liberal view to which it is ostensibly opposed—is often stated less moderately by communitarians such as Michael Sandel and Mary Ann Glendon,[11] for whom the domain of private life has been permitted to extend beyond its legitimate bounds by a pervasive political individualism. As with many of liberalism's critics on the left, communitarians would see the pendulum swing in the direction of public ends, if not eliminate the public/private distinction altogether.

A common tactic of many Marxist, socialist, communitarian, and other critics of the public/private dichotomy, and of the private sphere in particular, is to highlight several unfortunate consequences of privacy as it has traditionally been conceived, often leaving open the question of privacy's proper bounds or interpretation. It is relatively uncommon at present for social critics to call without further ado for an end to privacy. More commonly, attention is directed toward disparities in power or wealth or to some set of disutilities of which this principle is asserted to be the cause. As Charles Sykes states, "no one disparages privacy to its face. They simply choose to emphasize the public's right to know, national security, personal safety, conveniences, economic opportunity, politics, ideology, or the pursuit of virtue."[12] As if tacitly conceding legitimacy to one or another conception of privacy—even while awarding emphasis to values of a countervailing sort—often such critics leave unresolved or unaddressed the issue of the principle's proper interpretation and scope.

Among the critiques that take the concept of privacy itself to task is Judith Jarvis Thomson's skeptical challenge regarding the coherence and distinctiveness of this notion. For Thomson, positing a right to privacy serves no purpose since it is a right derivative from other rights already entrenched in law. "It is possible," Thomson maintains, "to explain in the case of each right in the cluster [of rights ostensibly comprising a general right to privacy] how come we have it without ever once mentioning the right to privacy. Indeed, the wrongness of every violation of the right to privacy can be explained without ever once mentioning it."[13] All purported violations of privacy, on Thomson's view, are either unobjectionable or objectionable on the grounds that they violate rights unrelated to privacy—specifically, property rights and rights over one's person. What is offensive, for instance, in the act of reading another's diary without their permission is that the act violates a right of property over the diary. Similarly, the intrusion of spying violates a right to security of the person. In these and all other cases of privacy invasions, Thomson asserts, the intrusion is fully explainable in terms of these prior rights, rendering a right to privacy otiose. Thomson further argues that the notion of privacy itself lacks any conceptual core that could explain its application across such disparate contexts as abortion and reproductive autonomy, interests in property and personal information, lifestyle choices, sexuality, and so on. These heterogeneous interests, she maintains, defy explanation in terms of a unitary principle. The notion of privacy is at best a composite of values and interests having little in common rather than a distinct moral category which could be brought to bear in resolving cases. The concept of privacy, accordingly, must be put aside in the interest of clarity.[14]

Still more formidable a challenge not only to the dichotomy of public and private but to the concept of privacy itself comes from feminist scholars who have documented the myriad ways in which traditional interpretations of privacy have concealed and legitimized forms of power which public institutions are incumbent to prevent. When, in the modern age, ancient assumptions regarding gender and male-female relations combined with liberal preoccupations with property, the idea gained new impetus that the private sphere—more specifically, the household—is a domain properly removed from public view and presided over by a dominant male. Yet, as feminists have so often pointed out, the domestic sphere is the site not only of individual retreat, family life, and private property but of inequality between the sexes, female servitude, and domestic violence. Catharine MacKinnon, to take one representative example, writes,

> The law of privacy treats the private sphere as a sphere of personal freedom. For men, it is. For women, the private is the distinctive sphere of intimate violation and abuse, neither free nor particularly personal. Men's realm of private freedom is women's realm of collective subordination.[15]

The point is echoed by Susan Moller Okin: "The protection of the privacy of the domestic sphere in which inequality exists is the protection of the right of the strong to exploit and abuse the weak."[16] Indeed, the observation is so often repeated in the feminist literature that the critique of privacy and of the public/private dichotomy could well be described as one of the central points, if not the central point, of feminist theory.[17]

The argument is perhaps familiar enough that I shall not need to rehearse it here in detail. In short, many feminists take the view that separating the public from the private removes from public view relations of superordination and subordination that are gender based, relations appropriately characterized as political. The sphere of the political extends beyond that to which liberals have traditionally assigned it—the state—to include power relations generally, including power within personal relationships and the domestic sphere. The feminist idea that "the personal is the political" constitutes a critique of efforts to immunize male-female relationships and the power operative therein from public scrutiny on grounds that such relationships are personal or occur in the home. Privacy becomes ideological when it is used to mask or to lend moral legitimacy to disparities in power that are rooted in gender. As well, the separation of public and private has served to legitimize assigning men and women to separate domains of social life, more especially to consign women to the domestic sphere by virtue of purportedly natural differences between the sexes.

This feminist argument—when stated in its moderate forms—draws few critics at the present time. It has essentially carried the day among political theorists, legislators, and an increasing number of the general public, feminist and nonfeminist alike. No longer does one hear serious individuals espousing the views that women ought not to be free to participate on an equal basis with men in the public domain, that domestic violence is a personal matter for which legal redress is unnecessary, or that a man is the unquestioned king of his castle. These archaic views were already coming into question in the nineteenth century, from nonliberal and liberal quarters alike. (One thinks of Mill's text *The Subjection of Women* as a case in point.[18]) What is controversial is less the persuasiveness of the feminist critique of the public/private dichotomy than the implications of that critique. Specifically, what becomes of the private sphere, and the distinction between public and private, when we concede the feminist argument? If these two realms of social life are no longer conceivable as radically opposed, must the distinction collapse altogether such that human affairs as a totality would fall under the unified category of politics, or "the political"?

Among radical feminists, the answer often appears to be that a distinction in any form—dichotomous or otherwise—is irredeemably ideological, from which it follows that a right of privacy or a private sphere in any form possesses no moral or political legitimacy whatever. I say "appears to be" since this rather troublesome conclusion is seldom stated explicitly in the literature. What receives explicit commentary most often is the argument's critical moment, while its positive implication remains ambiguous. MacKinnon, for instance, speaks bravely of the need for feminists to "explode the private,"[19] while leaving the implications of this maneuver largely unstated. What specific consequences for public policy follow from exploding the private sphere? Where, for example, does it leave feminist arguments for abortion which often speak of reproductive matters as covered under the privacy umbrella? (Indeed, it was precisely such an argument that the U.S. Supreme Court cited in its decision in *Roe v. Wade* to decriminalize abortion.) It is equally unclear exactly how seriously such declarations are meant to be taken. Whether the radical feminist proposal to explode the private is to be understood at face value or regarded as mere hyperbole is unclear, particularly to the uninitiated.

Jean Bethke Elshtain offers this rendering of the radical feminist claim:

> The claim is not that the personal and political are interrelated in important and fascinating ways previously hidden to us by sexist ideology and practice; nor that the personal and the political may be analogous to one another along certain axes of power and privilege, but that the personal *is* political. What is asserted is an identity, a collapse of the one into the other.[20]

Carole Pateman offers the same interpretation: "The most popular slogan of today's feminist movement is 'the personal is the political,' which not only explicitly rejects the liberal separation of the private and public, but also implies that no distinction can or should be drawn between the two spheres."[21] If this interpretation is correct, the radical feminist program calls for a thoroughgoing rejection of the private, leaving us with an undifferentiated political sphere.

If there is a single proposition to which all of these feminists would agree concerning the distinction between the public and the private, it is that the distinction as traditionally conceived has served to conceal or rationalize relations of power between men and women and that redressing the matter requires a fundamental rethinking of the relation of the personal and the political so that issues of gender inequality may see the light of day. It is a proposition to which most nonfeminists would likely also assent. Yet where the radical program collapses the public/private distinction altogether, other feminist and nonfeminist scholars prefer to redraw the boundaries or reconceptualize the distinction in ways that remove vestiges of ideology. Indeed, it is often feminist scholars themselves who argue most effectively on behalf of preserving private life from a potentially totalitarian public order. In related ways Judith Wagner DeCew, Patricia Boling, Jean Bethke Elshtain, Ruth Gavison, Anita Allen, Jean Cohen, and Janna Malamud Smith each defend a conception of the private which eludes telling criticisms of its traditional interpretations. Elshtain, for instance, writes,

> If there are no distinctions between public and private, personal and political, it . . . follows that no differentiated activity or set of institutions that are genuinely political, that can serve as common bases of order and purpose in a political community, exist. What does exist within such a collapse of public and private is a vision of pervasive force, coercion, and manipulation: power of the crassest sort suffusing the entire social landscape, from its lowest to its loftiest points. There are few alternatives in such a world: one is either victim or victimizer, oppressor or oppressed, triumphant or abject. Politics itself, as a differentiated sphere of human activity, disappears in this yearning for a totalistic solution to all human woes, a thoroughgoing fusion of all principles.[22]

If the injustices to which radical feminism seeks a remedy are forms of power that consign women to subordinate positions in social life, the remedy is unlikely to come in the form of a power more onerous and totalistic than what it would replace. As history regularly shows, a public order that reaches into every corner of human affairs gives rise not to relations of equality between persons but to a general suppression of human freedom and equality alike.

Along similar lines, Judith Wagner DeCew argues that feminism may challenge abuses traditionally rationalized by the principle of privacy without abandoning the principle itself; indeed, it is this very principle, appropriately conceived, that factors prominently in the critique of these same abuses. In her words,

> Feminists want to do away with the whole public/private dichotomy *as it has been understood in the past*. Thus feminists stress that they do not intend to have the state insinuating itself into the most intimate parts of people's lives. They are instead emphasizing that the state must stop ignoring the unbelievable abuses that have been protected in the name of privacy; this is, they believe, a position that is not captured by the public/private distinction as it has been known and used.[23]

It is not privacy itself, then, or the separation of public and private spheres that is the source of the problem but the ideological uses to which the distinction has been put—chiefly, the maneuver to conceal injustices rooted in gender from public scrutiny and legal redress by spurious appeals to a private domain (a variant of the tyrant's eternal refrain that how he treats his subjects is a matter of internal affairs). DeCew continues:

> Exploitation and abuse *should* be matters of public concern. But that need not imply that there is never value in making a distinction between public and private. We need not be committed to the view that there should be *no* limitations on state interference in individual, personal, and intimate affairs. We need not be pushed to agree that there should be *no* private realm within which women can live their lives free from state policing and intrusion.[24]

One is easily tempted into the view that the remedy to a given injustice is a pendulum swing to the antithetical extreme, a move that eliminates one injustice while invariably ushering in new injustices remarkably similar to the original. Removing all vestiges of privacy on the grounds that it is subject to abuse, as Anita Allen has pointed out, is rather like removing liberty on the same grounds.[25] Remedies of a more evenhanded variety, while less inspiring than radical politics, tend at the very least to approximate a more just condition or to create fewer problems than they solve. In this case a less radical remedy would be to redraw the boundaries between public and private and (a little more radically) to reconceive the distinction itself with respect to its theoretical meaning and rationale as well as its practical applications in light of the feminist critique.

Like all political values, privacy is far from an unmixed blessing. It secures a degree of liberation even as it casts a shadow which must not be ignored. If this shadow has been ably brought to our attention in recent decades, it does not follow that all matters of a hitherto private nature must become objects of unlimited public or state power. A better idea, as Patricia Boling suggests, is "not to make 'public' and 'private' into reified categories, their content fixed and immune to change or criticism, but see them instead as permeable realms of human life which change over time."[26] It is to conceive the distinction along pragmatic lines as a useful way of negotiating social reality and of determining whether given cases of decision making properly fall to individual agents or to the public at large. More specifically, it is to recall the fundamental purpose served by the appeal to privacy, which is not to oppress but to protect personal choice, whether the person in question be male or female.

It is precisely here that the ultimate lesson of the feminist critique comes into view. It is to remind us that the meaning and purpose of privacy consist not in relegating women to positions of social inferiority—a consequence of this principle's distortion—but in protecting areas of human life from unnecessary and unwelcome intrusion. The separation of public and private spheres is neither a fixed verity nor a hierarchical opposition reinforced by ancient prejudices regarding gender. Rather, it gives recognition to the need to differentiate areas of choice in the service of human freedom and equality. Where feminists remind us that the privacy of one gender has been enjoyed at the expense of the other, the remedy lies not in abolishing privacy but precisely in extending its application to include men and women on an equal basis. The injustice to which feminist criticism points is not that men have enjoyed too much privacy but that women have enjoyed too little, that private life for the latter has not been the scene of personal or intimate choice but of its absence. The appropriate remedy, then, is not to compound power upon power as the radical program entails but to extend privacy rights to all persons. Thus conceived, the feminist critique of privacy carries liberalism to its completion rather than overthrowing it in the manner that it is frequently conceived. It is a critique that in its measured form applies the principle of equal rights, including privacy rights, beyond where liberalism traditionally conceived of it and removes vestiges of paternalism which liberals themselves either failed to notice or regarded with equanimity.

It is only in its radical form that feminist criticism entails a new brand of political totalism, an undifferentiated public realm in which no limit is placed on the power of public institutions and public opinion. In its measured forms, such criticism reminds liberals and other students of politics that it is only by securing the rights of all that human freedom is attained. A public domain without limits is precisely what defeats the prospect of a social order that is both free and equal. It therefore follows, as Elshtain notes, that "to the extent that the public world, with all its political, economic, bureaucratic force, invades and erodes the private sphere, it, not the private world, should be the target of the social rebel and feminist critic."[27]

WHY PRIVACY?

It is regrettable that in this era of academic specialization political theorists seldom venture outside their liberal, communitarian, feminist, critical theoretic, or other discursive enclaves to engage in a meaningful way with those of other schools. Discourse inevitably ossifies when it turns so thoroughly inward toward small circles of initiated specialists, insiders, and fellow travelers that the outside world assumes an alien appearance, as such camps engage less in dialogue and mutual learning than in "political struggle." Liberal and feminist scholars, for example, are not known for the discursive virtue of speaking to, rather than about and past, each other or for the courtesy of gaining acquaintance with one another's literature. If too often liberals speak to other liberals about feminism while feminists return the favor, what would carry the argument regarding privacy forward are attempts at mutual learning and interrogation from two schools that have both gained profound insight into the conditions of a just society.

If liberalism is correct in identifying among these conditions respect for universal human rights and a distinction between public and private spheres, feminism is correct in pointing out distortions in the interpretation and application of these principles which have tended to hoist liberalism with its own petard. Overlooking or conferring legitimacy upon gender-based class structures gives the lie to the principle of equal rights while reducing by one half liberalism's celebrated defense of the individual. Feminist criticism compels liberalism toward a fundamental reconsideration of the distinction between public and private, to examine more deeply the significance and implications of this old distinction for persons of both genders and of diverse personal description. It is such a reconsideration that I undertake in this section.

I commence my argument by shifting ground somewhat from political theory narrowly conceived to the field of social ontology or, more simply, human relations. It is not a peculiarity of modern Western culture that human relations in both public and private settings are spontaneously regulated by tacit yet generally shared understandings regarding social distance. Interaction between persons is invariably governed in one fashion or another by preunderstandings regarding personal boundaries and personal space which play a role so elementary to moral consciousness as typically to escape our notice. As is so often the case with the more elementary phenomena of human understanding, we become conscious of these preunderstandings only as a result of their breakdown. Examples of such breakdown are familiar from ordinary experience. A conversation that takes place at high volume between individuals situated at opposite ends of a room while others party to a separate conversation stand between them constitutes a breakdown of the "rules" or unspoken "code" governing interpersonal interaction. The individuals located at opposite ends of the room are commonly said to be rude or to be demonstrating a failing of some minor sort. They are properly reminded that the people standing between them are having a conversation. By the same token, an interaction between two persons who are not on intimate terms that takes place at very close quarters for no reason that is compelled by circumstances beyond the control of either party constitutes a similar kind of breakdown or intrusion. There are persons who habitually take up space that exceeds what is due to them according to shared preunderstandings regarding personal space, while others (far fewer) occupy less than their due. A person who crowds, nudges, and shout-talks oversteps invisible boundaries in ways that demean and detract from the general civility, even if such overstepping does not in the usual course of things constitute a major violation of morality.

Yet major violations also have the characteristic of overstepping boundaries of the self. Physical and sexual assaults are extreme cases of personal boundary violations. Far deeper than the physical injury such assaults cause, as victims of violent crime often attest, is the psychological and moral indignity to the person. Violence violates not only the physicality of its victim but its very being. While its means are physical, its purpose is to demean, to strip away dignity and self-respect. We would not wish to understate the differences between the minor infractions mentioned here and the profound injustice of violence. Their differences are radical and plain to observation. However, reflecting on each of these instances from the point of view of personal boundaries and social distance raises questions concerning both the content of our preunderstandings regarding such distance and its general function in human relations.

If there is a tacit "code" governing social distance which can be stated concisely, it is that proximity—physical and psychological—between persons is contingent on the nature of the relationship between them and, more important for our purposes, is subject to the will of both persons on an equal basis. Respecting another means in part respecting boundaries of the self, practicing a certain forbearance in recognition of the other as a moral equal. Recognizing the sovereignty of the other with respect to matters of interpersonal proximity is one of the ways in which we give practical meaning to the notion of respect or dignity. Just as violence violates another's whole being, observing boundaries erected by another demonstrates respect for that individual's personhood. An actor oversteps boundaries in deciding for others what degree of proximity and manner of access to them one will acquire, for instance, or what intimate acts or situations one will observe.

Perhaps the most essential function of social distance is to shield areas of intimacy and the more profound aspects of life from invasions that have the effect of degrading much of what gives meaning to our existence. It is not always realized that the depths of life and the self are fragile constructions that require a degree of protection in order to be what they are. Profundity seeks distance from the public, the ordinary, and the readily accessible. It seeks shadows over the spotlight, just as intimacy seeks protection from prying eyes. To be what it is, the self must regulate what degree and kind of access others will have to it, which information or dimension of the personality it will reveal to whom. Intimacy that does not discriminate is not intimacy but its most profound distortion.

As Edward Hall has observed, one's sense of self is inextricably linked with a sense of space. He writes, "the realization of the self as we know it is intimately associated with the process of making boundaries explicit."[28] Self-realization crucially involves the freedom to grant or withhold access to oneself or the capacity to reveal or conceal aspects of one's being as one chooses. In so doing, one regulates the distance between oneself and others and decides freely into what interactions and relationships one will enter and on what terms. The distortion to human relationships and to personal dignity that occurs in the absence of social distancing is profound and well known. At the level of interpersonal relationships, for example, psychologists describe the incapacity to assert personal boundaries (an incapacity often rooted in abuse) as being fatal both to intimacy and to self-realization. At the level of politics, totalitarian regimes recognize no limit to the reach of public institutions into the lives of their subjects, with a profound loss of dignity and civility as inevitable consequences. The concentration camp is the extreme case not only of the violation of liberty but of the complete absence of personal boundaries and solitude. As Charles Sykes observes, "concentration camps strip humans of their dignity by stripping them of any tiny corner of privacy, where they can be undisturbed or unobserved. At Auschwitz, wrote Primo Levi, 'solitude in a Camp is more precious and rare than bread.'"[29] Overcrowding in prisons—one of the most frequently heard complaints from the incarcerated—is a less extreme example of this phenomenon. One could mention as well, to take an illustration from everyday life, the implicit "code" or imperatives that govern the very ways in which we look at people. While largely tacit again, this code is surprisingly elaborate and well understood at a pragmatic level. Beyond injunctions not to stare and to give "dirty looks," there are a great many social rules that prohibit and sanction ways of looking at other persons. To look through someone, for instance, as if they were not there may be profoundly demeaning to the person now compelled to entertain the possibility that he or she does not exist. Salacious looks both intrude and demean by overstepping personal boundaries and by confronting their "victims" with the perception of them as objects of sexual gratification and nothing more. A key premise of the feminist critique of pornography is precisely that consumers of pornography may become habituated to perceiving women in a degraded light, a perception that removes a barrier to violations of a more serious nature. There are looks that see too much or too little, that look in the wrong direction or in the wrong spirit. There are looks that covet, intimidate, or ridicule, as well as those that communicate respect or intimacy. Standards of appropriateness, while ambiguous, govern each of these with an eye to ensuring social peace and personal inviolability. Many other examples of this general phenomenon could be mentioned, but what they all illustrate is the profound indignity brought about by the absence of both social distance and the freedom to regulate that distance. The absence of social space diminishes the self and undermines civility in the same gesture.

One could even find analogies to this phenomenon within the animal kingdom where considerations of space are frequently all-important. Studies of animal behavior often demonstrate the importance to many species of periods of solitude and intimacy, the role of territoriality in self-preservation, the connection between aggression and overcrowding, and so on. Alan Westin notes, "the animal's struggle to achieve a balance between privacy and participation provides one of the basic processes of animal life. In this sense, the quest for privacy is not restricted to man alone, but arises in the biological and social processes of all life."[30]

Returning now to the field of politics, we can identify a vital connection between the function served by personal boundaries and social distance in the general sphere of human relations and the principle of privacy in politics. A right of privacy, I would suggest, is the political counterpart of these other human values and has its philosophical justification in much the same source. That source, or sources, are the simultaneous conditions of individual agency and civility or social peace. As I have argued elsewhere,[31] individual selfhood is not without certain conditions of possibility, some of which are manifestly political. Human rights in general constitute fundamental conditions of moral personhood rather than mere expedients to the greatest happiness. They constitute political recognition that one's existence is one's own and that all are free to participate in social life on a basis of moral and legal equality. These same conditions place civil association on a peaceful basis and place a burden of ethical justification on relations of power in their myriad forms.

In particular, a right of privacy secures persons against unwanted intrusions into areas of life that more profoundly touch on who we are and what meaning our lives hold for us. It creates a jurisdiction of personal choice within which one is free to experiment with conceptions of the good life which may be conventional or unconventional. It is not an accident of history that privacy has become a central topic of political discussion at a time when pressures toward social conformity and normalization reach ever more deeply into human lives. The popular sense that personal privacy is under threat is rooted not only in recent technological innovations and preoccupations with security but in a general culture of exposure and ubiquitous normalization. When the sex lives of presidents become not only a topic of public gossip but an ostensibly political issue, pressures upon presidents and the rest of us to conform to majoritarian values reach absurd proportions. As the possibility of refuge from public scrutiny, judgment, or embarrassment diminishes, the title to one's personal existence becomes a little less one's own. When majorities, confident in their assumptions, set about to surveil and counteract personal decisions by means of public opinion and public institutions, the impression takes hold that our lives are not in our hands, that individuality is circumscribed by powers and pressures toward normalization that can be remarkably difficult to resist. It is the sense of control over who we are that is imperiled when private decisions must be justified to others in terms they would accept.

Jeffrey Reiman speaks in similar terms of privacy as a political measure by which "an individual's moral title to his existence is conferred."[32] He writes,

> Privacy is an essential part of the complex social practice by means of which the social group recognizes—and communicates to the individual—that his existence is his own. And this is a precondition of personhood. To be a person, an individual must recognize not just his actual capacity to shape his destiny by his choices. He must also recognize that he has an exclusive moral right to shape his destiny. And this in turn presupposes that he believes that the concrete reality which he is, and through which his destiny is realized, belongs to him in a moral sense.[33]

It is instructive, as Reiman also observes, to conceive both of individual lives and of the self as "an ongoing social process,"[34] or as something that is not fixed in either a metaphysical or a moral sense. The person and personal life are continually in process of becoming what they are (as Friedrich Nietzsche would say) by fashioning and implementing decisions. The self is the creation of a process of self-realization that begins in crude form very early in life—in the form, for example, of achieving bodily integrity. Such integrity is one of the principal achievements of childhood, and it is made possible by (among other conditions) respecting boundaries of the self which include privacy. Inviolability is a condition of persons' becoming what they are.

One might ask whether it is not possible for individuals to become what they are in the public realm or in ways that are subject to public scrutiny. What, the critic might ask, does the advocate of privacy have to hide if not the desire to dominate others behind closed doors? This is an important question given that appeals to privacy, as previously noted, have often served precisely this purpose. Yet however legitimate the concern underlying this question is, it remains that the sphere of private life is of profound psychological, ethical, and existential importance and reaches far deeper than the will to tyrannize. Private spaces are not merely where we carry out those actions that we would be ashamed to commit in full view of others but are the appropriate abode of several of the more existentially meaningful areas of human life. Intimate relationships, experiments in personal self-creation, and creative undertakings of various kinds occur in private as a matter of some necessity. As Hannah Arendt observes, "there are things that need to be hidden and others that need to be displayed publicly, if they are to exist at all. If we look at these things, . . . we shall see that each human activity points to its proper location in the world."[35] Practices and activities of many kinds are often accompanied by imperatives that their agents may not ignore: artistic expression requires periods of solitude before a work is presented to an audience, at which time the work—in order to be a work of art—requires a public audience; romantic love requires the retreat of two people from the public environment in order to become an actuality; the processes of dying and grieving require periods of solitude so that one may come to terms with the reality of death or loss. It is a common feature of many matters of profound personal or existential importance that they take place in private and away from everyday pressures of normalization.

Private life is the natural abode of experimentation and creative energies of various kinds. By definition, an experiment is an activity or a choice in which the outcome is unknown and which remains for this reason a probationary matter. It does not enter the public domain until its author witnesses its result and either endorses it as his or her own or rejects it as a failure. One must take a chance, yet when the public gaze is trained upon one, such chances become measured in light of the omnipresent threat of public censure. "If we have to think that everything we do is observed and may be publicized," as Ruth Gavison writes, "we shall have . . . less of a tendency to do the things that we are not sure about, fewer chances to experiment and acquire competence through trial and error, and fewer opportunities to experiment with behaving differently."[36] It is a commonplace that we learn largely within a process of trial and error—particularly error—and that when opportunities for this diminish, something of fundamental importance to the self is lost with it. What is lost are opportunities to fashion a point of view that is authentically one's own, one that has benefited from experiments both successful and unsuccessful and from mistakes one has learned not to repeat. What is also diminished is the idea of the human being as, in Warren and Brandeis's phrase, an "inviolate personality."[37] Unwelcome intrusions into private life diminish the personality or integrity of the self, considerations far deeper than injuries to reputation or emotional distress which are also frequent consequences of such intrusions.

What is more, while the desire for privacy is readily mistaken for "antisocial" desires to hide or to tyrannize over another, it is worth noting that sociability itself presupposes as a matter of necessity the possibilities of both retreat and secure possession of that which one would share with others. A "deeper, more chosen openness," as Janna Malamud Smith observes, is premised on the possibility of aloneness.[38] It is the freedom to withdraw and to withhold that makes participation in its various public forms possible. Liberality, to take one example, would not be possible were it not for the right to private property; one cannot share what one does not possess. Similarly, in private life friendship and intimacy presuppose an inviolate self which one voluntarily shares with another. It is only because of secure possession that we are able to relinquish or share anything at all. Charles Fried writes, "the man who is generous with his possessions, but not with himself, can hardly be a friend, nor—and this more clearly shows the necessity of privacy for love—can the man who, voluntarily or involuntarily, shares everything about himself with the world indiscriminately."[39] Sociability in general—if it is to be both peaceful and free—requires as a condition of possibility a degree of unsociability.[40] The social and the unsocial, the interpersonal and the personal, the public and the private are not antithetical values but dialectical counterparts.

In the general field of social ontology there is often a spontaneous logic or proto-logic at work which, while ambiguous, permits of a degree of phenomenological description. Human relations both public and private contain implicit conditions, limits, and principles without which we would be reluctant to characterize such relations as "human." Classical liberals described the breakdown of these conditions as the state of war, escape from which constitutes the principal motive of civil association. The social contract was to inscribe in law the fundamental conditions of both social peace and individual agency—it being understood (however imperfectly) that the conditions of the one are the conditions of the other. The distinction between public and private spheres has its basis in a social ontology for which civil peace and autonomous individuality are mutually entailed. Social justice is constituted neither by the triumph of the individual over the social nor by the reverse but by a recognition of the dialectical co-relativity of these values.

While defending the rights of the private sphere belongs to the individualistic pole of this dialectic, it is ultimately the dialectic itself—the dynamic tension of public and private, communal and individual—that, if successfully negotiated, creates the conditions of a just order. If at present the reach of public institutions and the public gaze more generally extends rather far into human lives, it is the sphere of private life that must reassert itself. Ultimately, it is the principle of respect for persons that entails not only a right of privacy but human rights generally. All such rights are properly conceived as guarantors of individual inviolability or means by which respect for persons—meaning all persons regardless of gender, age, race, ethnicity, and so on—is inscribed in law. What specifically the right to privacy protects is the social distance alluded to earlier. If it belongs to the notion of personhood to be not only a member of the social whole but a particular individual or self, respecting persons means respecting the distance between persons and the ethical and legal constraints whose purpose it is to protect this distance. While this does not entail a conception of individuals as asocial atoms, it does incorporate a view of the person as more than an appendage of the social organism. The person is at once a citizen—a participant in public life and a social being in all aspects of its existence—as well as an individual, a distinct and potentially autonomous agent. It is as both public citizen and private individual that the principle of respect entails the rights of the person.

Efforts to locate human rights within a more general conception of respect and human dignity are familiar to students of political theory. Immanuel Kant's efforts to this end are particularly well known, while in recent times theorists such as Julie Inness, Stanley Benn, Charles Fried, and Jeffrey Reiman have applied similar deontological argumentation to privacy rights.[41] Benn, for instance, defends the view that "respect for someone as a person, as a chooser, [implies] respect for him as one engaged on a kind of self-creative enterprise, which could be disrupted, distorted, or frustrated even by so limited an intrusion as watching."[42] Benn attempts to ground privacy on the principle of respect for persons conceived in conventional liberal terms as rational choosers, while Inness defends a less orthodox view of "respect for persons . . . as beings with the capacity for love, care, and liking, as well as rationality. Thus, we value privacy because it embodies our respect for persons as autonomous loving, caring, and liking beings."[43] It is mistaken, then, to hold that privacy or individual rights generally presuppose social atomism as a matter of logical necessity. It presupposes only that the respect due to individual bearers of rights is due to them as distinct or separate persons no less than as citizens in the public sphere.

It bears emphasis that the social distance of which I have been speaking is a condition not only of individual agency—a traditional preoccupation of liberal individualists—but of civility or social peace. Intuitively, privacy appears to belong among political values of an essentially individualistic sort. It protects the individual from the public institutions and social masses which threaten to overstep their limits and violate boundaries of the self. Yet personal privacy is no less a condition of values of an essentially "social" nature. Political regimes that recognize no limit in principle to the public domain are almost by definition uncivil societies. Their pure form is the totalitarian state, while their kinder and gentler forms include the society that pries, scrutinizes, and exposes at will the details of private life.

On a scale of everyday life, we have no difficulty in recognizing the cost to civility that would result were everyday privacies to be systematically overstepped. A society without walls, locked doors, and personal boundaries is a scenario that no sane person would wish to defend. Yet the cost to social peace brought about by prying institutions, an array of small powers, and a culture of exposure is becoming increasingly visible and problematic. While utilitarian grounds often exist for the kinds of public overstepping of which I am speaking (as the following chapters discuss), the immediate utilities they bring about are offset by a general deterioration of social life and diminution of civility.

Liberalism has always understood, after a fashion, that public and private interests are not pursued in isolation but that each is a condition of the other. This thesis finds expression, to take a familiar example, in classical liberal economics, wherein the private interest in financial gain leads by an "invisible hand" to the public good of prosperity. The social contract as well establishes a conception of the common good as obtained only under conditions of individual freedom. Civil association is brought about by institutions and legal measures that optimally protect the freedom of all. While without question liberal theorists and legislators have not always carried this principle into practice in a meaningful way, it remains an insight of liberal philosophy that public and private values are pursued together or not at all.

In the particular case of privacy, this view is expressed in the claim that privacy rights are simultaneous conditions of individual agency and civil association. Public involvements of every description presuppose an inviolate self no less than do undertakings of a purely personal nature. Privacy does not merely isolate individuals from the public realm but provides the normative structures that enable persons to participate in social involvements in their various forms.[44] It forms part of a general fabric of rights that in their totality constitute a framework for social peace and civility no less than does private well-being. Here again the analogy with nonpolitical everyday life readily suggests itself: interpersonal relationships of every kind presuppose as a matter of psychological and moral necessity obligations to respect another's privacy together with related considerations of personal space. Friendship or intimacy is inconceivable apart from such conditions, when no limit exists to the psychological and physical intrusion of another or when the threshold of what constitutes an intrusion is not subject to the will of the individual.

Proponents of the right to privacy, as of any right, must account not only for its legitimating rationale but for its limits as well. If there is reason to distinguish public and private domains, what limit exists to the sphere of private life or to the right of privacy, a limit that provides initial clarification to the relation between these two realms of social life? Here I would suggest, in the tradition of John Locke and John Stuart Mill, that the concept of harm defines the limit upon the right of privacy and the private sphere. Acts in other respects private cross into the public domain when they inflict harm or injury upon an individual who is not the performer of the act. It is the obligation of public institutions to intervene under this circumstance and not under more general circumstances entailed by the principle of utility, paternalism, or related standards.

What has come to be known as the harm principle was articulated in the seventeenth century by Locke in the following terms: "The part of the Magistrate is only to take care that the Commonwealth receive no prejudice, and that there be no Injury done to any man, either in Life or Estate."[45] In the nineteenth century, Mill would express the same principle that injury or harm is the only basis of legislative intervention into private affairs and the basis in principle of the public/private distinction: "the only purpose for which power can be rightfully exercised over any member of a civilized community, against his will, is to prevent harm to others. His own good, either physical or moral, is not a sufficient warrant."[46] The limit of privacy rights is identified by that which establishes their necessity—the imperative of personal security or inviolability as a condition of moral agency and social peace. Private acts that harm or violate the right of another require constraint since these conditions are no longer met.

In practical terms the harm principle creates a provisional assumption that within the sphere of private life persons are at liberty to pursue self-chosen ends by self-chosen means and that individuals or institutions that would compel them to act otherwise must justify their action in specific normative terms. Specifically, such justifications must appeal to the principle of harm and identify which rights of which persons are overstepped by acts that in other respects are private. This working presumption, then, places an onus of justification on prima facie intrusions into private life while delimiting the terms such justifications must take. It removes the burden from individuals to justify private acts by reasons acceptable to the general public or its institutions in the same way that the right of free speech removes the burden of moral justification for particular speech acts. Their general rationale, as of all free acts that do not cause harm, lies in the conditions stated here: they are measures by which persons become what they are, make their lives their own, and give meaning to their existence without violating others' rights to do the same. Beyond this, it is not incumbent upon persons to justify private choices. In particular (as I have cause to argue in several contexts in the chapters that follow), it is not incumbent upon them to account for private acts by appealing to majority opinion, custom, or the general happiness. It is in the removal of such burdens that the liberating potential of privacy may be seen.

DEFINITIONS AND ISSUES

Philosophers and legal theorists are far from agreeing not only upon the value of privacy but upon its conceptual meaning. The search for definitions necessarily begins by saving the phenomena of language and noting the disparate uses of the term *privacy* in both political and nonpolitical settings. As many have noted, this seemingly simple endeavor quickly becomes anything but, raising the question whether privacy as a moral category possesses any coherence whatever, whether it is perhaps reducible to something else or is irredeemably confused. As mentioned, Judith Jarvis Thomson has defended the reductionist thesis that privacy is wholly derivative from the rights to property and security of the person and that apart from such prior rights privacy lacks conceptual coherence. The reductionist thesis is not one that I propose to defend, nor do I proffer any kind of essentialist core to the concept of privacy. If we wish to save the phenomena of this term's disparate uses, the most that can be hoped is that we gain an approximate working understanding of privacy as it functions in social criticism and ordinary language. If the notion of privacy does not admit of a set of necessary and sufficient conditions governing its use, neither are its designations merely a random assortment of claims and interests. In this respect privacy is hardly unusual among the more elementary terms of normative appraisal. Fairness, equality, and democracy are only a few such terms that, while serving indispensable functions within moral and political discourse, admit of only an impressionistic understanding. (I have argued elsewhere that the essential ambiguity of many such terms is not a cause for regret but on the contrary is a necessary condition for semantic innovation and other purposes of social criticism.[47]) If, accordingly, it is an impressionistic understanding that we seek, a satisfactory one will both incorporate the disparate uses of privacy as well as "help us to understand," as James Rachels puts it, "what makes something 'someone's business' and why intrusions into things that are 'none of your business' are, as such, offensive."[48]

On the view I propose, privacy violations in their various forms are experienced as invasions—and as offensive—for the reason that they constitute negations of personal meanings and self-conceptions by which human beings live. If it is by meanings that we live and move and have our being, such meanings and self-understandings are violated in large ways and small by everything that counts as an invasion of privacy. If we consider the disparate examples of what are asserted to be privacy violations—everything from eavesdropping to voyeurism, invasive questions, meddlesome institutions, and so on—what they appear to have in common is an overstepping into areas of an individual's life that are intimate or personal in the sense that they touch upon deeper meanings at the heart of one's self-understanding as a separate person. There are a few points here that require elaboration.

First, from an external, analytic vantage point there are likely no common elements uniting all cases in which privacy significantly factors into the analysis. The common dimension that these cases share is visible from only a phenomenological and participatory standpoint of individual agents engaged in life projects of various kinds. From an experiential vantage point, privacy delimits areas of one's personal existence over which one claims a right of self-determination on grounds of their immediate connection to self-conceptions and meanings commonly described as personal. Even as such values sustain an individual through life, ultimately they are contingent and fragile constructions in need of psychological and moral protection precisely for this reason. When that by which one lives (or a sizable share of it) is both self-fashioned and frailer than we sometimes imagine, psychological and normative structures are needed to render inviolable that which in being violated is destroyed. Fundamental meanings and self-conceptions are as inviolable as the persons whose lives they orient, and it is for this reason that boundaries delimiting the personal and the intimate emerge spontaneously in social life in the form of tacit imperatives and preunderstandings governing social distance. It is this general area of life that Mill somewhat awkwardly described as the "self-regarding," a domain of conduct bearing immediately and directly upon the agent and hence a matter of private concern.[49] While Mill's distinction between self-regarding and other-regarding action has not withstood examination with success, the underlying intuition that it expresses remains significant. It is that it is imperative, morally and psychologically, for persons to claim a right of self-determination over choices so fundamental to our being that to be deprived of them is experienced as a violation. Privacy infractions not only unduly restrict our field of action but, more fundamentally, violate our being in a manner analogous to violations of personal boundaries.

Second, it is our integrity and identity as individuated selves or as small groups of persons that are at stake in privacy cases, rather than our identity as citizens. If it is characteristic of the public body (*res publica*) to assert a right of collective self-determination extending to all matters of common concern to persons in their public capacity as citizens, a comparable right of personal self-determination governs cases in which our identity as separate persons prominently factors. One distinguishing feature, then, of privacy contexts is that they invariably bear upon matters of "personal" concern or issues that affect one as an individual or intimate group of individuals rather than as participants in larger forms of communal life. The status of the person—whether one is acting in the role of citizen or in the personal capacity of friend, spouse, or parent—features prominently in the distinction between public and private.

Attempts to define privacy more strictly invariably fail to do justice to the term's hermeneutic richness. Authors of such definitions typically award exclusive attention to particular connotations of privacy which appear to be of relative importance, consequently neglecting other shades of meaning that do not fit within the definition. One example of this is a proposal to define privacy strictly in terms of information about individuals. Alan Westin, for instance, restricts the scope and meaning of privacy to "the claim of individuals, groups, or institutions to determine for themselves when, how, and to what extent information about them is communicated to others."[50] Given the contemporary importance of information privacy and, more generally, the fact that it is an age of information into which civilization is headed, it is unsurprising that efforts to define privacy narrowly often focus, no less narrowly, upon information and its circulation in the public domain. Yet the large number of connotations and denotations of privacy in everyday speech that are unrelated to the matter of information render this definition unduly narrow. Undoubtedly, a satisfactory account of the meaning and scope of privacy will include an important place for informational issues, but as is often the case when strict and narrow definitions of familiar normative concepts are sought, the "clarity" that such a definition affords is purchased at a prohibitive cost—that of neglecting too many connotations of the term that circulate in ordinary language. It is not information that the voyeur seeks, nor is it what is gained and lost when a closed door is abruptly opened to the horror of the persons behind it. In these cases it is the fact of being seen, quite apart from the information that being seen imparts, that constitutes the violation. It is being exposed, seen in an embarrassing or compromising circumstance, but above all being seen against one's will that makes such cases privacy violations. When a patient's medical or psychiatric file is read without the patient's knowledge and consent, and without a legitimate medical purpose, the act constitutes an overstepping of boundaries and an intrusion into the personal, again quite apart from the information that the file contains. Such an act involves no violation of property rights, or of a right to security of the person, but a distinct form of overstepping.

Doing justice, then, to the hermeneutic richness of this term entails recognizing an important element of relativity in the meaning of privacy, even as its meanings relate and overlap in the fashion of a family resemblance. The explanation of its relativity lies in the fact that the personal meanings and self-understandings with which the sphere of the private is concerned are variable qualities. Indeed, the most illuminating account of privacy may well be its most colloquial: it is that which is "my business" or what is "personal" in the sense that it is intimately bound up with who the particular person is. Since what is personal is by definition relative to the person, there are no fixed parameters of the private, no objective criteria of the inherently private. To a large extent, "my business" is what I deem it to be: it is particular items of information about myself that I wish not to be circulated without my consent; it is actions and interactions with intimates that they and I do not wish for public display; it is meanings by which I live, whether these meanings are widely shared or peculiar to myself. The important matter of the threshold that distinguishes privacy violations from lesser intrusions is not altogether fixed but is contingent on how and where individuals establish boundaries.

Were it not for political and legal purposes, relativity would constitute one of the principal characteristics of the realm of the private. These purposes, however, compel us to draw lines straighter than they would otherwise be. Since laws necessarily apply to all, fashioning them occasionally requires a certain hermeneutic imposition of solidity on what by its nature is fluid, as privacy law well illustrates. Accordingly, if harm constitutes the limit of privacy or the threshold between privacy violations and transgressions of a lesser order, the sort of harms or injuries that define this threshold are necessarily those that permit of a level of generality among persons. Not only are these transgressions unwelcome, but they are reasonably expected to be unwelcome and to cause harm or injury to their victims. Such harms may be subtle or unsubtle, ranging from the loss of personal security to the shame of exposure, to the restriction of options beyond what is rightfully one's own. In this last respect privacy transgressions may resemble in their consequences violations of liberty where the harm done is no physical injury but the elimination of choices that belong, or ought to belong, to all persons. Ultimately, the harm that privacy violations cause is to remove or diminish the title one holds over one's existence and personal affairs.

This last point brings into view privacy's close connection to another fundamental category of political discourse: liberty. The similarity between these two values—with respect to definition, philosophical justification, and practical application—will be clear to all. It is what distinguishes them that calls for description. What I would propose, to state the matter concisely, is that while cases involving privacy and liberty frequently overlap, the distinction between them turns on the quality of intimacy or the personal which may be present in cases involving liberty but which is morally salient in privacy contexts alone. Where liberty bears more generally on decisions affecting one's life, privacy's content centers on decisions and matters of an intimate nature. As Julie Inness states, the scope of privacy "ranges over decisions concerning intimate access to the agent, intimate information about the agent, and intimate actions on the agent's part."[51] Privacy's definition and scope are not limited to informational matters, particular actions of the person, or access to the person but encompass all three. Such a view accords closely with intuitive conceptions of the private and with its various uses in social criticism and ordinary language.

Recalling feminist criticism of the public/private distinction, and in particular of the ideological function that appeals to a private sphere have served, it bears emphasis that the conception of privacy here proposed is not reducible to the domestic realm, to family life, or to property. The spatial connotation of privacy refers not to any physical domain—the domain of the home or of property more generally—but to a moral space surrounding the person. Metaphorically, privacy is a "portable territory" of the self, analogous in this respect to personal space.[52] It is not an enclosed domain within which one may oppress another with impunity, nor is it a realm that one enters or exits. It is a right of personal security broader in both its meaning and its application than the familiar right to "security of the person" (primarily the right against physical assault). Accordingly, the scenario of the domestic tyrant claiming immunity from public intervention on grounds of privacy or private property is met with a compelling reply. Injustices arising from power relations in the home or within interpersonal relationships are not immune to public intervention and legal redress, on the grounds that such relationships are personal or on any other basis. The limit of the personal is the harm caused to another and the transgressing of boundaries that the other rightfully determines.

However important the distinction between public and private is for purposes of social criticism, it is a distinction that is far from straightforward in either its abstract meaning or, still more, its practical applications. If the argument to this point has demonstrated the importance of a private sphere and provided initial clarification to its scope and meaning, further clarification is required regarding the implications of the distinction within different areas of public policy. To what in particular does a right of privacy extend, and in what ways does it help us to navigate several of the more contested issues of our time? Privacy has factored prominently in debates concerning such disparate issues as the dissemination of information, access to electronic files, abortion and contraceptive practices, drug testing and drug laws, sexual morality, domestic life, child rearing, and others. Determining on which side of the public/private distinction each of these issues falls assists efforts of social critics and legislators to fashion policy options in these areas, even if this determination itself is both contestable and far from constituting the last word on the subject. This determination provides a key premise from which these and related issues may be approached.

Adding to the complexity of determining which issues are privacy issues is the hybrid nature of many institutions of civil society and the number of issues or areas of social life that comprise aspects of both public and private. The distinction with which we are concerned is neither categorical nor fixed in nature but comprises boundaries that are shifting and uneven. It is a complexity that is evident as well from uncertainty on both the left and the right regarding privacy's scope and from the confusing array of positions that each side has adopted on the general matter of the public and the private. While the left has traditionally favored considerable public involvement in areas of economic and social policy, it typically resists similar involvement in issues of conscience, abortion, sexual morality, and free speech. Conservatives reverse these positions, yet by no evident logic does the passion for privacy or for liberty exhibited by both sides prevail in one set of issues and not the other. Conservatives typically favor free economies and private property yet an unfree conscience and a conformist public morality. Apart from appeals to tradition or "consensus," conservatives lack any principled basis by which to distinguish public from private issues. The left fares no better in this regard, advocating a free conscience yet an unfree economy and public institutions that are invasive and burdensome. What this illustrates is that the issue of privacy does not revolve exclusively around the axis of left and right and that when it does so revolve, it does so by fiat.

I have argued that the principled basis of the distinction between matters of personal self-determination and majority decision lies in normative imperatives arising from conditions of individual agency and social peace. Identifying the implications of this general hypothesis for several of the issues listed here is the task of the chapters that follow. The topics on which I have chosen to concentrate are both pressing and far-reaching in their consequences for public policy, although several other issues in which privacy prominently factors are hardly less important. The following chapters follow no necessary order. They are thematically overlapping yet relatively freestanding investigations which seek to negotiate an old and embattled distinction.

NOTES

1. As Stanley Benn observes, "Over the last century or so, public authorities—whether through regulatory agencies or the courts—have come increasingly to restrict individuals' options in order to prevent their doing themselves harm or knowingly entering into arrangements by which others might harm them, and have aspired to promote their good in more positive ways as well, irrespective of their own wishes. Examples of such interference are seat belt and safety helmet legislation, control over the sale of dangerous drugs, compulsory prophylaxis of various kinds, and enforcing safety standards on manufacturers, thereby preventing consumers from choosing cheaper but riskier products. True, the object of the regulation is not always the individual's own well-being alone; some public interest may also be involved (compulsory vaccination is a case in point). In the case of protective clothing and seat belts, however, the well-being of the subject himself does seem to be the dominant consideration, even if a supplementary case could be made out in terms of the use of scarce medical resources; and it is doubtful whether even in the other cases public rather than individual protection loomed largest in legislators' minds." Benn, "Private and Public Morality: Clean Living and Dirty Hands," in *Public and Private in Social Life*, eds. Stanley Benn and G. F. Gaus (New York: St. Martin's Press, 1983), 176–77.

2. Jean Bethke Elshtain, *Public Man, Private Woman: Women in Social and Political Thought* (Princeton, N.J.: Princeton University Press, 1981), 22.

3. See, for instance, Hannah Arendt, *The Human Condition* (Chicago: University of Chicago Press, 1958).

4. Prominent defenders of this view include John Stuart Mill and Friedrich A. Hayek. As the latter writes, "in a truly free society, public affairs are not confined to the affairs of government (least of all central government) and public spirit should not exhaust itself in an interest in government." Hayek, *Law, Legislation and Liberty*, vol. 2, *The Mirage of Social Justice* (Chicago: University of Chicago Press, 1976), 151.

5. G. F. Gaus and Stanley Benn express this point as follows: "Liberalism is committed to the protection of the individual's conscience and projects; and when his beliefs and plans are unpopular, this commitment translates into a defence of the individual from the pressures of public opinion. The tendency of liberals to applaud an independent minority who refuse to bow to the pressure of public opinion sometimes stems, as in de Tocqueville and J. S. Mill, from a disparagement of the masses as a 'collective mediocrity'; but liberals are also prepared to support the rights of a misguided minority who shun the true beliefs embedded in public opinion. Because the liberal places a value on independence and self-direction, he is always apt to be wary of public or mass opinion which might undermine these virtues by producing an unreflective conformity." G. F. Gaus and Stanley Benn, "The Liberal Conception of the Public and the Private," in Benn and Gaus, *Public and Private in Social Life*, 36.

6. Samuel Warren and Louis Brandeis, "The Right to Privacy," in *Philosophical Dimensions of Privacy: An Anthology*, ed. Ferdinand David Schoeman (Cambridge: Cambridge University Press, 1984), 76.

7. James Fitzjames Stephen, *Liberty, Equality, and Fraternity* (New York: Henry Holt, 1873), 160.

8. Jean Cohen, "Rethinking Privacy: Autonomy, Identity, and the Abortion Controversy," in *Public and Private in Thought and Practice: Perspectives on a Grand Dichotomy*, eds. Jeff Weintraub and Krishan Kumer (Chicago: University of Chicago Press, 1997), 143.

9. See John Stuart Mill, *On Liberty* (New York: Norton, 1975).

10. Amitai Etzioni, *The Limits of Privacy* (New York: Basic, 1999), 4.

11. See Michael Sandel, *Democracy's Discontent: America in Search of a Public Philosophy* (Cambridge, Mass.: Harvard University Press, 1996); Sandel, "Moral Argument and Liberal Toleration: Abortion and Homosexuality," *California Law Review* 77, no. 3 (1989); Sandel, "Religious Liberty—Freedom of Conscience or Freedom of Choice?" *Utah Law Review*, no. 3 (1989); Sandel, "The Procedural Republic and the Unencumbered Self," *Political Theory* 12, no. 1 (1984); Mary Ann Glendon, *Abortion and Divorce in Western Law* (Cambridge, Mass.: Harvard University Press, 1987); and Glendon, *Rights Talk* (New York: Free Press, 1991).

12. Charles Sykes, *The End of Privacy* (New York: St. Martin's Press, 1999), 8.

13. Judith Jarvis Thomson, "The Right to Privacy," in Schoeman, *Philosophical Dimensions of Privacy*, 287. H. J. McCloskey argues along similar lines that "any right to privacy will be a derivative one from other rights and other goods." McCloskey, "Privacy and the Right to Privacy," *Philosophy* 55 (1980): 17–38.

14. Arguments for the nondistinctiveness of privacy have also been presented by Richard Posner, "An Economic Theory of Privacy," in Schoeman, *Philosophical Dimensions of Privacy*; William Prosser, "Privacy," in Schoeman, *Philosophical*

Dimensions of Privacy; and Frederick Davis, "What Do We Mean by 'Right to Privacy'?" in *South Dakota Law Review* 4 (1959).

15. Catharine MacKinnon, *Toward a Feminist Theory of the State* (Cambridge, Mass.: Harvard University Press, 1989), 168.

16. Susan Moller Okin, *Justice, Gender, and the Family* (New York: Basic, 1989), 174.

17. Some other representative exponents of the feminist critique of privacy are Carole Pateman, Iris Young, Patricia Boling, Shulamith Firestone, and Jean Bethke Elshtain.

18. See John Stuart Mill, *The Subjection of Women*, in *On Liberty and Other Writings*, ed. Stefan Collini (Cambridge: Cambridge University Press, 2003). Other nineteenth-century writers that one might note in this connection are Karl Marx, Friedrich Engels, Charles Fourier, and Saint-Simon.

19. MacKinnon, *Toward a Feminist Theory*, 191.

20. Elshtain, *Public Man, Private Woman*, 217.

21. Carole Pateman, "Feminist Critiques of the Public/Private Dichotomy," in Benn and Gaus, *Public and Private in Social Life*, 295.

22. Elshtain, "The Displacement of Politics," in Weintraub and Kumer, *Public and Private in Thought and Practice*, 172.

23. Judith Wagner DeCew, *In Pursuit of Privacy: Law, Ethics, and the Rise of Technology* (Ithaca, N.Y.: Cornell University Press, 1997), 90.

24. DeCew, *In Pursuit of Privacy*, 89.

25. Anita Allen, *Uneasy Access: Privacy for Women in a Free Society* (Lanham, Md.: Rowman & Littlefield, 1988), 40. More recently, the same author appears to have reversed course, now arguing that "we are accountable for the best candidates we have for harmless and self-regarding conduct (for example, consensual oral sex between monogamous partners in their own bedroom). We do not simply face others' 'advice, instruction, persuasion, and avoidance'—devices Mill approved. We face social and legal demands for sanctions and other reckoning he disapproved. Mill's assertion that individuals are 'not accountable to society' for actions that concern only themselves is debatable as a matter of ethics or political morality and flatly inaccurate as a matter of fact. Not only are we held accountable for what is commonly termed private life, but our accountability for some personal, arguably self-regarding, conduct extends to the extreme of criminal liability." Allen, *Why Privacy Isn't Everything: Feminist Reflections on Personal Accountability* (Lanham, Md.: Rowman & Littlefield, 2003), 2. She also now cites with approval the following remarks of Andreas Schedler: "In our private lives we wade in a constant stream of accountability initiatives. People hold their children, parents, partners, friends, neighbors, colleagues, and fellow citizens accountable for any kind of presumptive misbehavior—for political incorrectness, insubordination, disorderliness, bad memory, drinking and smoking, sexual misconduct, sinful behavior, lack of courtesy, strategic errors, factual ignorance, whatever. Because there are lots of rules that guide our private lives, there are lots of opportunities for private agents of accountability to step in and monitor and enforce compliance." Schedler, "Conceptualizing Accountability," *The Self-Restraining State*, eds. Andreas Schedler, Larry Diamond, and Marc Plattner (London: Rienner, 1999), 2.

26. Patricia Boling, *Privacy and the Politics of Intimate Life* (Ithaca, N.Y.: Cornell University Press, 1996), 15.

27. Elshtain, *Public Man, Private Woman*, 333.

28. Edward Hall, *The Hidden Dimension* (Garden City, N.Y.: Doubleday, 1966), 11.

29. Sykes, *End of Privacy*, 19.

30. Alan Westin, "The Origins of Modern Claims to Privacy," in Schoeman, *Philosophical Dimensions of Privacy*, 59.

31. See Paul Fairfield, *Moral Selfhood in the Liberal Tradition: The Politics of Individuality* (Toronto: University of Toronto Press, 2000).

32. Jeffrey Reiman, "Privacy, Intimacy, and Personhood," in Schoeman, *Philosophical Dimensions of Privacy*, 310.

33. Reiman, "Privacy, Intimacy, and Personhood," 310.

34. Reiman, "Privacy, Intimacy, and Personhood," 310.

35. Arendt, *Human Condition*, 73.

36. Ruth Gavison, "Too Early for a Requiem: Warren and Brandeis Were Right on Privacy vs. Free Speech," *South Carolina Law Review* 43, no. 3 (1992): 461.

37. See Warren and Brandeis, "Right to Privacy." Edward Bloustein provides an informative discussion of "inviolate personality" in "Privacy as an Aspect of Human Dignity: An Answer to Dean Prosser," in Schoeman, *Philosophical Dimensions of Privacy*.

38. Janna Malamud Smith, *Private Matters: In Defense of the Personal Life* (New York: Addison-Wesley, 1997), 8.

39. Charles Fried, *An Anatomy of Values: Problems of Personal and Social Choice* (Cambridge, Mass.: Harvard University Press, 1970), 142.

40. I have argued this point at some length in *Theorizing Praxis: Studies in Hermeneutical Pragmatism* (New York: Lang, 2000), chap. 5.

41. See Julie Inness, *Privacy, Intimacy, and Isolation* (New York: Oxford University Press, 1992); Stanley Benn, "Privacy, Freedom, and Respect for Persons," in Schoeman, *Philosophical Dimensions of Privacy*; Benn, "Private and Public Morality"; Charles Fried, "Privacy," in Schoeman, *Philosophical Dimensions of Privacy*; Jeffrey Reiman, *Critical Moral Liberalism: Theory and Practice* (Lanham, Md.: Rowman & Littlefield, 1997); and Reiman, "Privacy, Intimacy, and Personhood."

42. Benn, "Privacy, Freedom," 242.

43. Inness, *Privacy, Intimacy, and Isolation*, 11.

44. Ferdinand Schoeman defends a similar position in *Privacy and Social Freedom* (Cambridge: Cambridge University Press, 1992). Also see Robert Murphy, "Social Distance and the Veil," in Schoeman, *Philosophical Dimensions of Privacy*.

45. John Locke, *A Letter Concerning Toleration* (Indianapolis, Ind.: Hackett, 1983), 42.

46. Mill, *On Liberty*, 10–11.

47. See Paul Fairfield, *The Ways of Power: Hermeneutics, Ethics, and Social Criticism* (Pittsburgh, Pa.: Duquesne University Press, 2002), chap. 4.

48. James Rachels, "Why Privacy Is Important," in Schoeman, *Philosophical Dimensions of Privacy*, 292.

49. Mill, *On Liberty*, 10–11.

50. Alan Westin, *Privacy and Freedom* (New York: Atheneum, 1967), 7. Richard Wasserstrom, William Parent, and Elizabeth Beardsley similarly define privacy rather narrowly in terms of personal information and its uses. See Wasserstrom, "Privacy: Some Arguments and Assumptions," in *Philosophical Law*, ed. Richard Bronaugh (Westport, Conn.: Greenwood, 1978); Parent, "Recent Work on the Concept of Privacy," *American Philosophical Quarterly* 20 (1983); Beardsley, "Privacy: Autonomy and Self-Disclosure," in *Privacy*, Nomos 13, eds. J. Roland Pennock and John Chapman (New York: Atherton Press, 1971).

51. Inness, *Privacy, Intimacy, and Isolation*, 140.

52. Robert Sommer, *Personal Space: The Behavioral Basis of Design* (Englewood Cliffs, N.J.: Prentice-Hall, 1969), 27.

Chapter Two

Privacy in an Age of Information

Understanding normative categories and distinctions in theoretical terms provides initial clarification to their meaning, yet for purposes of both theoretical understanding and social criticism further clarification is required in the form of particularized analysis of their applications and how these enable us the better to understand and negotiate social reality. The distinction between public and private is no exception to this, illustrating on the contrary that both the distinction itself and the right of privacy are inseparable ultimately from the manner in which they are brought to bear on matters of practice. The theoretical focus of chapter 1, accordingly, is replaced in chapters 2 through 4 with a concentration on issues in which privacy claims factor prominently. Each of these studies endeavors to come to terms with the essential ambiguity of the public/private distinction and to put the distinction to work in a fashion that does not overlook its contested and dialectical quality. In preserving and negotiating such ambiguity, the approach of these studies in effect reverses the premise of mainline normative theories that principles must be known clearly and distinctly prior to their practical applications and prior as well to the practice of social criticism which employs such categories. My premise (which I have discussed elsewhere at greater length[1]) is that normative principles, including privacy rights and the separation of public and private spheres, are never comprehended in this fashion but require for their intelligibility concrete determination in particular acts of criticism.

It is, then, a transition of sorts, from theory to practice, that the following three chapters undertake. In each the ambiguity of the distinction at a theoretical level of analysis is mirrored on the level of practice. It is an ambiguity that social criticism must cope with and in some measure overcome, even as its capacity to do so is not without limits. The questions this chapter raises pertain to the meaning and implications of privacy rights in an age of science-technology and, more specifically, in an age of information. The global civilization that is upon us is characterizable in a variety of ways, yet one that permits of little controversy is that the present era of globalization is an era of technology and information, these two values being intimately related. A variety of ethical and political questions stems from this, including not least the implications of technological power for social life generally conceived and for human rights in particular. What is the future of human freedom in an age of science-technology and, more specifically, of rapidly advancing information and communication technologies which make infringements of information privacy remarkably easy and indeed commonplace?

While the broad question of the impact of modern technology upon human rights has been with us for some time, philosophical efforts to come to terms with this issue have not matched the pace of technological advance. On the specific question of information privacy, traditional ethical theories appear largely silent, if indeed they are not irrelevant altogether, leaving commentators and legislators with little by way of principled guidance and a list of issues of increasing urgency and number. Whether a utilitarian, Kantian, or intuitionist treatment of such issues would be either determinable or useful is eminently doubtful. Moreover, as I have noted, these are not issues that revolve neatly around the axis of left and right, most especially in the case of information privacy in which socialists and conservatives are as likely to find common cause as not. Adding to the complexity is that the normative distinction of greatest relevance to the problems before us—that between public and private—contains a sizable gray area into which these issues appear to fall. Information privacy relates to the circulation of personal information within public and professional domains, information of varying degrees of sensitivity or significance to individuals.

In navigating these waters, I argue that the public/private distinction provides an indispensable interpretive perspective upon the ethics of information privacy and that this theoretical distinction and the practical matter of personal data protection are mutually illuminating. In particular, this chapter seeks to apply a general right of privacy to the issue of personal data protection. In pragmatic terms, what does a right of information privacy entail? What legislative measures and principles appropriately limit the uses of personal information by organizations that increasingly rely on its availability and transmission within public domains? How do we separate trivial or necessary intrusions from the more objectionable privacy violations that are increasingly coming to public attention? Like many questions of public policy, the questions before us are of more than passing philosophical significance and a significance that transcends a straightforward "application" of formal principles. Larger questions of technology and power provide a philosophical background for the specific issues that concern us here, some of which questions I examine in due course. I also discuss briefly several legislative measures that a variety of North American and European jurisdictions have adopted over the past few decades that are relevant to our discussion.

THE EMERGENCE OF A PROBLEM

Public concern over the decline of various forms of privacy—including *personal information privacy*, a term that Alan Westin (as previously noted) defines succinctly as "the claim of individuals, groups or institutions to determine for themselves when, how and to what extent information about them is communicated to others"[2]—began to emerge toward the end of the nineteenth century and increased steadily throughout the twentieth. The expansion in scale and number of both public and private institutions is among the leading causes of this phenomenon, institutions that through the course of the twentieth century became increasingly reliant on information in ever-enlarging quantities. Toward the end of the century, institutions and their publics had become mutually dependent to an unprecedented degree, with the appetite of such institutions for personal data seemingly insatiable and with their publics becoming increasingly habituated to the disclosure of such information.

Alongside a general habituation to disclosure has emerged a growing unease and uncertainty regarding its practical necessity and the uses to which such information may be put. As public agencies (e.g., law enforcement and intelligence, health care, tax collection, immigration, education, public records) and private organizations (e.g., media outlets, insurance companies, banking and credit institutions, labor unions, and professional groups) have generally assumed a more pervasive presence in the social landscape, the invasiveness of institutions into personal lives has steadily increased. Coupled with this are impressive advances in technologies of information collection, storage, communication, and manipulation, of which such institutions make regular use. While practices of surveillance and record keeping were hardly unknown before the latter decades of the twentieth century, the advent of computerization dramatically altered their scope and efficiency. For the first time it became possible to compile comprehensive individual profiles by merging disparate files without an individual's knowledge, making seemingly innocuous disclosures far more troublesome than those once offered in an era of manual record keeping. As dependence upon institutions has increased, decisions regarding people's fate depend ever more on institutional estimations of persons and their needs, capacities, proclivities, or health as determined by information that persons may or may not freely supply. As one sociologist remarks,

> Surveillance has spilled out of its old nation-state containers to become a feature of everyday life, at work, at home, at play, on the move. So far from the single all-seeing eye of Big Brother, myriad agencies now trace and track mundane activities for a plethora of purposes. Abstract data, now including video, biometric, and genetic as well as computerized administrative files, are manipulated to produce profiles and risk categories in a liquid, networked system. The point is to plan, predict, and prevent by classifying and assessing those profiles and risks.[3]

Surveillance technologies have also greatly assisted news reporting and entertainment concerns that nourish public appetites for embarrassing personal disclosures from "public figures" and ordinary citizens alike. As media outlets provide a regular diet of scandal, corruption, or their "perception," a corresponding perception has it that all alike are vulnerable to privacy violations of increasing scale.

As recent decades have witnessed a veritable explosion in information and information technologies, the notion of an information age has quickly entered the public consciousness and affected profoundly our understanding of the present and anticipations of the future. Information and knowledge, economists tell us, have surpassed labor and capital as the driving force of modern economies. Business transactions, institutional reckonings, and the fate of persons increasingly turn upon information and the fashion in which it is collected and arranged, be it by individuals or computers. As one commentator describes the information age,

> More transactions will tend to be recorded; the records will tend to be kept longer; information will tend to be given to more people; more data will tend to be transmitted over public communication channels; fewer people will know what is happening to the data; the data will tend to be more easily accessible; and data can be manipulated, combined, correlated, associated and analyzed to yield information which could not have been obtained without the use of computers.[4]

Without doubt, the information age into which modern civilization has moved is neither altogether auspicious nor inauspicious in its implications. Like the age of science from which it is directly descended, the information age is ethically neutral, at once securing in many respects a more optimal weight of utilities over disutilities while simultaneously creating new kinds of dangers, several of which fall under the privacy rubric.

Several of these dangers are coming increasingly to general attention as well as the attention of legislators in many nations. They include the issue of access to electronic files containing sensitive personal information or information that is voluntarily disclosed under one set of circumstances and subsequently transferred without the individual's knowledge or consent. The relative sensitivity of personal facts is often contingent upon the conditions surrounding their original disclosure, including the voluntary or involuntary nature of the disclosure, the persons to whom the disclosure was made and their roles, the reasons and timing of the disclosure, and so on. Private disclosures made in a physician's or psychologist's office under conditions of a specific professional relationship that are later accessed by agencies with nontherapeutic interests, or indeed interests directly contrary to the subject, raise privacy concerns that are often far more serious than the embarrassment that may result. At the present time, as the number of files on each of us continues to expand, access to them becomes progressively uncomplicated for a variety of agencies and individuals. Employers, insurance companies, credit and financial institutions, investigators, landlords, and a host of public institutions enjoy ready access to personal information from people who may not have authorized (or knowingly authorized) its release or who revealed it to specific persons with an expectation of confidentiality.

The problem of access is compounded by the fact that information is often more readily gained by agencies or by persons other than the subject than it is by the subject him- or herself and by the fact that the subject does not typically realize the number and location of files that exist. A person intent upon accessing every file that exists on him or her faces a formidable challenge, while access by the wrong persons, whether overt or covert, is often remarkably easy. Further, aside from investigators, few realize the extent of information that has been gained about them and by whom. As one observer notes,

> The individual rarely realizes the number of records held by city, county, state, and federal agencies that are open to investigators and anybody else for public inspection. These may include police arrest blotters, civil and criminal court records, motor vehicle accident reports, records of driving convictions, and possibly even welfare rolls or other records involving contacts with social service agencies. This information is available legally in most cases. Where it is not legally accessible, other means may be used by some investigators.[5]

Information in files may be inaccurate or obsolete if not regularly updated; it may be incomplete or distorted due to the requirements of computer programs or forms that permit a narrow range of answers to standardized questions; and it is rarely destroyed, even after the purpose for which it was originally collected no longer remains. When such files are readily accessible, the possibility of compiling lists and individual profiles for a range of purposes is significantly enhanced, particularly given software programs designed specifically to abstract and compile data from disparate sources in a systematic way. The compilation itself affects the interpretive arrangement in which information is registered, transforming facts innocuous on their own or in their original context into a more damaging frame.

Finally, the invasiveness of many requests for personal information is a growing cause for concern both in its own right and in view of the frequency with which institutional decisions affecting a person are based on information gained in questionable ways. The census questionnaire represents for many a symbol of the presumption of many institutions to extract information about individuals for purposes unrelated to their personal well-being. The scope and rationale of the contemporary census have expanded dramatically from its original purpose of counting populations to one that now includes a host of questions and purposes that have the appearance of serving the ends of states rather than those of persons. Sensing this, a growing segment of the population has come to regard the census as the symbol of privacy's decline, although the insurance or credit application form, and many similar inquiries, might serve the same purpose.

This constellation of problems prompted most postindustrial states to adopt some form of information privacy or data protection legislation beginning in the 1970s. America's Privacy Act of 1974 serves as a case in point. Among its provisions, the act established a right of individuals to inspect and correct errors within all files concerning them held by federal agencies, proscribed secret personal information records, prevented data collected for one purpose from being shared without an individual's consent, and created a privacy protection commission to investigate abuses in both the public and the private sector. Like many other laws of its kind, however, the Privacy Act established only a limited scope for data protection and has generally failed to catch up with the rate of advance in surveillance and information technologies; furthermore, it did not establish adequate means by which citizens would be informed of their rights. Over three decades after the Privacy Act came about, it remains that

> American law generally presumes that individuals lose their privacy interests in particular information once they voluntarily disclose that information in any public setting. Our government's seemingly insatiable appetite for collecting information, combined with public access laws that tend to underplay the value of privacy, means that a great deal of personally identifiable and potentially sensitive data is automatically considered public information. Moreover, [American] laws are relatively inattentive to the secondary use of those data by the private sector. We are more inclined to treat each person's privacy in the sphere of commerce merely as an economic good to be protected or not by market forces.[6]

Identical concerns in European and other nations have prompted similar legislative efforts. The most important of these is the Council of Europe Convention on Data Protection of 1981 as well as the European Community Data Protection Directive of 1995. The provisions of these texts have provided the principled framework of national legislation throughout Europe. Not unlike the earlier American law, the convention guidelines stipulate that personal data must be lawfully obtained, accurate and up to date, relevant to the purposes for which they were collected, and not utilized for unrelated purposes. The guidelines provide a series of measures relating to the collection and storage of data, limitations on its uses, security provisions, and accountability, all in recognition of growing public concerns about databanks and the uses to which personal data may be put.

Difficulties regarding the enforceability and limited scope of such legislation as well as the continuing emergence of new technologies prevent data protection laws from being the panaceas for which legislators in many nations may wish. Government efforts to combat the drug trade, terrorism, and other security threats exert additional pressures upon values of personal and group privacy, pressures that show no signs of abating in the foreseeable future. Accordingly, the current prognosis of information privacy is decidedly mixed as increasing public attention and legislative efforts are matched by increasing threats. The predicament of states compelled to weigh each of these concerns is an unenviable one and one that the social critic or theorist is in no privileged position to remedy. Any principled framework that would assist current privacy debates will necessarily and uneasily coexist with security measures in particular, a consideration hardly less pressing than requirements for data protection.

If social criticism can offer no ready solutions to the general predicament described here, it can afford a more comprehensive understanding of the problem itself and how it came to pass and of the principles in light of which appropriate judgments might be made. Philosophical theorizing regarding technology, information, and power does not remove the necessity of practical judgment in weighing and applying normative imperatives that at times conflict. What it may do is provide an interpretive and ethical frame in which particular judgments may be made.

TECHNOLOGY, INFORMATION, AND POWER

When Martin Heidegger aptly described modernity as an age of "science-technology," he was describing not only the pervasiveness of technological gadgetry in contemporary civilization or the impressive rate of advance in scientific knowledge but, more fundamentally, the way in which "science-technology" (for Heidegger, a unified phenomenon) had become the definitive mode of presentation of being itself, a totalizing and quite inescapable way of ordering the world to the exclusion of other ways of thinking and interpreting. What comes to our awareness outside the interpretive frame of science and technique belongs no longer to the order of knowledge but to subaltern realms of discourse or affectivity. Technology has become so pervasive in the modern world that one can neither genuinely choose nor opt out of it; it has claimed us—our thought, our experience, our self-understanding—in a manner that is at once dangerous and ineluctable.

As the scientific method has come to stand as the veritable definition of knowledge, technology is increasingly the medium of social life as well. Political judgments and ethical relations alike are played out within a conceptuality of instrumentality and strategic use-value for which utilitarianism and contractarianism serve as exemplars. In the age of science the fate of persons and populations depends ever more on the strategic calculations of institutions and technicians, the intentions of which may be beneficent or oblique but whose estimation of subjects is seldom a trivial matter. Persons come to stand in the world as "standing-reserve," or resources to be pressed into service for technological and institutional purposes. If technology expresses and signifies a certain "will to mastery," as Heidegger believes, it is a will that "threatens to slip from human control"; the technological apparatus that ostensibly serves us gradually loses its character as a means and takes on the appearance of an end in itself, one to which we ourselves stand ever more as means. As he expresses it,

> Only to the extent that man for his part is already challenged to exploit the energies of nature can this revealing which orders happen. If man is challenged, ordered, to do this, then does not man himself belong even more originally than nature within the standing-reserve? The current talk about human resources, about the supply of patients for a clinic, gives evidence of this.[7]

Within this general picture, advanced information technologies and the information age as a whole are readily at home. Institutional mechanisms for determining needs, resources, benefits, or profit potential require information in ever-enlarging quantities and in a multiplicity of forms as necessary means of achieving institutional ends, whether these be profits or public service. In the process, a vocabulary of efficiency, administration, and functionality gains prominence. Persons lose the appearance of individuality and become populations, human resources, bearers of needs, or materiel in the general apparatus of mass society. As such, their needs, functionality, proclivities, and personal past must be recorded and communicated to agencies with similar information needs.

While the social reality that emerges is scarcely as repressive as innumerable regimes of the past, a variety of ethical problems have become especially recalcitrant in modern times owing to their profound roots within scientific-technological ways of thinking that unto themselves are neither ethical nor unethical. The benefits of modern technology are so undoubtedly many that it would be patent nonsense to call for a return to a prescientific age of belief or practice. Yet notwithstanding this, a growing sense of unease accompanies the proliferation of information and surveillance technologies together with invasive news reporting and ubiquitous demands for personal disclosure. As if set upon by an array of well-meaning but meddlesome inquiries, the modern subject finds itself endlessly obliged and available to whatever agency presents itself as requiring knowledge about it. This phenomenon is symbolized by the "public figure" or celebrity hounded by reporters and beset by demands for public exposure, yet a subtler and more pervasive condition finds the individual available to inspection by an array of officials, professionals, and technicians. As Deckle McLean writes,

> We have to put up with having our lives detailed in tax, police, medical, insurance, education, and credit data banks; on top of this, the news media will not give us room to cry alone when we are sad, or to buy groceries and go to the bank without the whole community being informed of our habitual itineraries, or to come to terms with flood damage without being made an object of the public's capricious sympathy.[8]

While the issue is easily overstated, there is an emerging public anxiety that however innocently intentioned many demands for personal disclosure may be, it is the ubiquity of this demand, its frequent intrusiveness, and the presumption with which it is made that make this phenomenon an insidious one. The discomfort follows upon a general sense of visibility or hypervisibility from which escape is seldom an easy matter. It follows as well from the fact that contemporary forms of hypervisibility are incompatible with visibility in its more genuine forms. It is not, after all, as a whole being or "existing individual" (as the existentialists would say) that one is encountered in such instances but as a need bearer, a functionary, a subject. Recognition of particularity under these conditions is in rather short supply, a complaint regularly encountered in contemporary culture. It is precisely the nonrecognition of particularity—of the self as an unrepeatable individual or member of a particular grouping—that aligns hypervisibility more closely to invisibility than to genuine visibility and that in the process exerts a subtle diminishing effect on subjectivity.

It must be asked, however, of exactly what variety or degree of harm privacy intrusions of this order are the cause or indeed whether they are necessary or even minor disutilities offset by the innumerable benefits of modern life. What distinguishes trivial irritations from real harms, and are critics of contemporary information practices merely quibbling about what in the final analysis is a minor issue? Large institutions on which we increasingly rely, after all, require information about their publics in order to deliver services with optimal efficiency. Their business is not to "recognize" persons in their particularity or "otherness" but to provide tangible benefits such as credit, insurance, education, medical care, or security. One may argue that surrendering control over personal data is a small price to pay for the benefits brought about thereby, an argument that already found considerable purchase prior to September 11, 2001. Since then, antiterrorist legislation such as the U.S. Patriot Act has further eroded personal privacy and related civil rights protection, conferring upon law enforcement agencies unprecedented powers of surveillance and arrest. This law—introduced with tremendous haste and passed with remarkably little debate just six weeks after the attacks—includes a plethora of legislative changes that dramatically increase the powers of law enforcement and intelligence agencies to gain access to personal information, monitor private communications and Internet use, conduct secret searches, expand the scope of subpoenas, seize library and bookstore records, and a variety of other activities that ostensibly serve the goal of national security and without the usual system of checks designed to protect civil liberties.[9]

The odd juxtaposition of what can only be described as patriotic hysteria which found expression in this controversial law with, for example, the tenor of President George W. Bush's 2005 inaugural speech, in which freedom was boldly proclaimed as America's world historical mission, is the more remarkable for being so seldom observed. Not since the McCarthy era has America witnessed such conservative hysteria as what has followed upon the events of September 11, 2001. Nor is it only politicians who have, unsurprisingly perhaps, been affected by this hysteria. Some political theorists as well have remarked upon this law in surprising, even naive, ways. One prominent communitarian, for instance, writes, "In the weeks that followed September 11, the country pulled together. A strong spirit of community prevailed. Bipartisanship governed. Differences were not suppressed, but they were worked out. Posturing was replaced largely by a competition for who could do more and better for the nation by working with the other side. Congress—working with the White House—sorted out where the new point of balance would be between our all-too-evident need to enhance public safety (especially facing the threat of terrorists using weapons of mass destruction) and our profound commitment to respect and uphold our rights."[10] It is highly doubtful that this is an altogether apt description of the spirit that prevailed in Washington and elsewhere in the immediate aftermath of September 11. Consider as well the following remarks by another prominent theorist: "Lincoln's unconstitutional acts during the Civil War show that even legality must sometimes be sacrificed for other values. We are a nation under law, but first we are a nation. I want to emphasize something else, however: the malleability of law, its pragmatic rather than dogmatic character. The law is not absolute, and the slogan '*Fiat iustitia rat caelum*' (Let justice be done though the heavens fall) is dangerous nonsense." As well, "if it is true, therefore, that the events of September 11 have revealed the United States to be in much greater jeopardy from international terrorism than had previously been believed . . . it stands to reason that our civil liberties will be curtailed. They should be curtailed, to the extent that the benefits in greater security outweigh the costs in reduced liberty."[11] Such sentiments call to mind Hobbes's oft-repeated refrain that the price for security is freedom. When politicians, in the heat of the moment, resort to draconian measures, it falls to social critics and theorists to call such actions by their name rather than allow themselves to be swept up in hysteria.[12]

As long as the vocabulary of utility and disutility is brought to bear on this issue, we shall tend to misdescribe the phenomena and mistake their ethical significance. Like many values, privacy does not readily lend itself to the language of cost-benefit analysis, and when it is examined in this frame, distortions quickly arise. I have identified here a constellation of problems regarding possible misuses of data, problems regarding their accessibility, accuracy, relevance, and so on, yet understanding the harms involved requires that we look further and deeper than practical interests of this order.

Michel Foucault well described the general manner in which modern social institutions subject persons to the possibility of total visibility and how such hypervisibility functions as a mechanism of power. The hypervisible subject, Foucault observed, becomes an agent of his or her own subordination, using Jeremy Bentham's Panopticon as a metaphor.

> He who is subjected to a field of visibility, and who knows it, assumes responsibility for the constraints of power; he makes them play spontaneously upon him; he inscribes in himself the power relation in which he simultaneously plays both roles; he becomes the principle of his own subjection.[13]

The Panopticon stands as a symbol of power mechanisms that employ surveillance, clinical scrutiny, or the omnipresent possibility of these as instruments of control. Subjects in the guardhouse of the Panopticon may be seen at any time and are aware of this. What they are unaware of is whether they are being watched at any given moment, forcing them into an identification with their guards and a reflexive consciousness that constrains their field of action.

With Foucault's analysis in mind, Jeffrey Reiman describes the effects upon privacy that total visibility brings about:

> We have privacy when we can keep personal things out of the public view. Information gathering in any particular realm may not seem to pose a very grave threat precisely because it is generally possible to preserve one's privacy by escaping into other realms. Consequently, as we look at each kind of information gathering in isolation from the others, each may seem relatively benign. However, as each is put into practice, its effect is to close off yet another escape route from public access, so that, when the whole complex is in place, its overall effect on privacy will be greater than the sum of the effects of the parts.[14]

The totally visible subject is the totally available subject—available for the purposes of the viewer, whatever they may be. When the availability of the subject for public inspection is total, and this by no choice of its own, it is the fact of its general visibility that acts as a mechanism of social control, apart from whether or how a given subject is actively scrutinized at a given moment.

Self-reflection in its baser, more neurotic forms is a predictable psychosocial consequence of the loss of information privacy. The lesson of the Panopticon is that persons who experience themselves as being completely visible inevitably succumb in large ways or small to imperatives of normalization and social conformity. When everything about one is known, or knowable, one's disposition to stand out from the mass faces a powerful opposition and in the usual instance is an imprudence. The subject's self-perception is transformed to match the perceptions of an anonymous other or a general public whose judgments are unknown to the subject but tend to be of the highest importance. Its actions and even its inner life are brought into conformity with the mass without the necessity of overt manipulation. What is lost, as Reiman states, is

> the inner personal core that is the source of criticism of convention, the source of creativity, rebellion, and renewal. To say that people who suffer this loss will be easy to oppress doesn't say enough. They won't have to be oppressed, since there won't be anything in them that is tempted to drift from the beaten path or able to see beyond it.[15]

It is well known that power and knowledge are intimate acquaintances, and in an age of information, power and information are hardly less so. Quite aside from the practical misuses of data to which I have referred, their widespread availability poses a subtler threat to the dignity of persons. Human dignity is threatened not only by overt rights violations but through the omnipresent potential for this. As with privacy, dignity is bound up with a sense of inviolability in one's agency and being, with assurances that means of protection from harm and legal redress are available. It is a sense that is threatened by ubiquitous scrutiny from without and vigilant self-scrutiny alike. As persons become increasingly accustomed to surveillance, everyday privacy violations, and demands for information disclosure that we comprehend neither the need for nor the purposes for which it will be used, small boundaries essential to social peace and respect are progressively encroached upon.

As a case in point, consider the practice of "outing" gays and lesbians and the profound disrespect that this involves. Irrespective of the motives of those who publicize such information against the subject's wishes, the significance of this act is the fashion in which it oversteps boundaries of the self and demonstrates in the process a disposition to violate boundaries more fundamental still. The outer declares the outed a subject of purposes not its own, a means toward a political agenda to which it may or may not subscribe. The act forces an alteration in the self-consciousness of the subject. Henceforth it is the perceptions of others that hold sway, that challenge the subject's self-understanding and profoundly alter its sphere of action. Outing announces a right of the general public to preside over the subject as the seat of justice and the determiner of fates. Aside from the general dubiousness of such perceptions—perceptions founded upon a single fact, taken henceforth as morally salient and determinative of character—is the indignity of depriving the subject of any quarter from hostile or unwelcome perceptions that compel an alteration of self-perception.

In related, if subtler, ways it is the condition of persons generally in an information age to be vulnerable to power mechanisms that employ personal information and perception to alter the self-understanding and sphere of action of individuals. If the consciousness of self is no longer overwhelmed by the scrutinizing gaze of the Creator or any centralized agency of power, it is now hedged about by an array of petty scrutinizers, each with apparently innocuous information needs, yet the net effect of which is profound. It comprises small, even petty, yet ubiquitous expressions of disrespect the more troubling for their ostensible necessity and profound roots within the order of science-technology. It comprises as well the frequently encountered disposition to overstep in large ways or small, to take liberties or merely to "get the goods" on someone. In this regard it is almost immaterial whether the goods in question are one's own or a stranger's; it is the disposition itself that unnerves us. It is never known precisely how information will be disseminated or used, in what direction public scrutiny will turn, what boundaries of civility or respect will be crossed, but merely that one is vulnerable. As small barriers against manipulation or public hostility are removed, the sense of personal inviolability is correspondingly attenuated.

Perhaps it is not an accident of history that baser forms of self-reflection which stem from a sense of hypervisibility and vulnerability take hold in a technological age. Does not the will to mastery, as Heidegger remarked, belong to the essence of technology as it bears upon the material and social orders alike?[16] Empirical investigation of the natural environment involves a certain epistemological imposition of form—a subsumption of phenomena within a theoretical frame or picture; only within this totalizing frame do the phenomena have intelligibility. Only through their availability to empirical inspection do phenomena possess a share of being. As much as new or anomalous data are explained in the usual course of science by being assimilated within existing empirical models, subjectivity gains a standing in social reality by taking its place within an institutional order, through its availability to inspection and mechanisms of normalization. In both spheres control and the will to mastery belong to technology's essence.

Here again the question arises whether there is not something inherently unjust about technology itself or social structures that reflect it, and again the question is appropriately answered in the negative. What I am describing are imperatives and dangers that are inherent to a scientific-technological order yet that do not for all that constitute a refutation or devastating critique of technology itself. Everything, as Foucault would say, is dangerous, and power is indeed ubiquitous. The task of social criticism is not to prophesy a time in which either might be eliminated entirely but to comprehend in a fundamental way the dangers inherent to the present and to identify principled means by which to cope with them. The principal danger of the present age of technology and information, that in which many lesser dangers have their source, is a disposition and an orientation that is the essence of technology itself. This is a disposition and orientation of control—not the domination of any centralized agency but smaller and ubiquitous mechanisms of power of the kind described by Foucault. These are powers dispersed throughout a network of institutional and professional structures, powers of scrutiny and expertise the more dangerous for their ostensible utility. If the condition of modern subjectivity is to find itself implicated within mechanisms of power, it is a power that is exercised upon all and monopolized by none. It is a power as well that accentuates values of adaptation over creativity—adaptation to a general apparatus of efficiency and strategic maximizing.

A symptom of this is what is often referred to as the *technological imperative*. This is the imperative, seemingly inherent to technological systems, to make optimal use of the latest advance, to become caught up in an endless proliferation of gadgetry, and to adapt oneself to its requirements. As much as we design technology for human purposes, we use it as it itself demands to be used, within parameters so narrowly circumscribed that the line between user and used begins to blur. "Using" advanced systems of technology, and learning how to use them still more, no more resembles using a paint brush or a snow shovel than complying with directives. The parameters of human activity and language itself increasingly reflect a kind of technologic in which legitimacy is measured by the yardstick of efficiency, innovation, or mere newness.

In understanding the dangers inherent to contemporary methods of personal information gathering we get to the heart of the matter in examining such techniques from the standpoint of imperatives that characterize information disclosures within ethical relations. In the usual course of social life, disclosures of personal information are spontaneously guided by norms or structures that are tacit yet broadly understood (or preunderstood). First, we reveal information not indiscriminately but to select persons and in a fashion that is piecemeal and contingent both on the relationship and on another's initial reception of particular items of information. Personal disclosure presupposes a level of trust between persons that is proportionate to the sensitivity of the facts being shared. Disclosure is a reciprocal communication or a process in which information is divulged by one party in relative proportion to another's disclosure. By necessity in ethical relations, disclosure is a matter of volition on the part of two or more parties. It is also a matter involving the confidence of both parties that sensitive information will not be revealed to third parties without the consent of the subject of the information.

Further, personal information disclosure tends to occur within a specific interpretive form. It is within a narrative structure that one reveals particular facts about oneself, whether it be in the context of recounting the general story of one's life or a specific episode within it. The disclosure of an isolated fact apart from any narrative context reveals remarkably little about the subject of the revelation or, at the very least, raises more questions than it answers. Consider, for instance, the circumstance in which one reveals without further ado that one has declared bankruptcy. Without emplotting this within a story—one possibly of considerable complexity—it is an isolated and virtually unintelligible occurrence, one that in itself reveals nothing of significance about the person. It defies understanding until it is situated within a narrative account of how and why it came about, the general circumstances surrounding it, when it occurred, its significance and consequences, and so on.

Finally, this form of disclosure belongs to a larger process described by G. W. F. Hegel as the dialectic of recognition. This is the well-known dynamic in which the self-consciousness of two parties is confirmed in a struggle for recognition. Mutual recognition constitutes the resolution of the struggle, as consciousness of self on the part of either party without the confirmation of the other is inherently contradictory. The revelation of personal information belongs to this process and is governed by its imperatives. The subject of disclosure has an investment in the manner of presentation as well as the reception of particular facts, their presentation serving as confirmation of one's self-understanding. Rarely is their presentation a matter of indifference to the subject of the disclosure. Rather it belongs to the project of negotiating self-conceptions and gaining recognition as the person one takes oneself to be. This negotiation, however, is far from a simple matter of utilitarian economics. What is "optimized" is the mutual recognition of the parties only, the imperatives in play all tending toward this outcome. It little resembles the buying and selling of products that characterize contemporary information commerce. Little more does it resemble the kind of information disclosures that typify our interactions with institutions.

The contrast between the kinds of self-construction operative within ethical relations and contemporary methods of information gathering is stark. In the latter instance, it is now possible (and, in fact, remarkably easy) through the accumulation of disparate items of information regarding a given individual to fashion a relatively detailed profile of that person.[17] A self fashioned by this means is the implied subject of a credit history, an educational background, a medical or psychiatric history, a criminal record, and similar information garnered from an array of files. It is a decidedly antinarrative self, one constructed from the outside in, as it were. It is also a self that stands in no obvious relation to the real person who bears the same name. Effectively the person is divided into two parts in a new kind of technological metaphysic: a virtual self, constituted by abstract informational bits arranged and assorted by means of computer programs for purposes of administrative efficiency, and the flesh-and-blood organism to whom the virtual self is ostensibly related—if not by identity, then epiphenomenally or by preestablished harmony. What is more, the fate of the "real" person—or indeed its reality—is increasingly contingent on institutional or public estimations of its virtual twin. For practical purposes, the "real" person is overtaken by the virtual; the former is onto-technologically demoted to the status of informational substratum or ghost in the machine. As Irma van der Ploeg remarks, even the seemingly self-evident distinction between the body itself and information pertaining to it may need to be questioned: "We may need to consider how the translation of (aspects of) our physical existence into digital code and 'information,' and the new uses of bodies this subsequently allows, amounts to a change on the level of ontology, instead of merely that of representation."[18]

Further points of contrast between personal disclosure in ethical relations and modern information-gathering techniques are equally plain. For the latter, disclosure is neither founded on trust, reciprocal, nor necessarily volitional. It proceeds within terms determined by the recipient of data rather than the individual to whom it belongs, including the form in which information is revealed and its quantity. Tacit imperatives that minimize the vulnerability associated with personal disclosure and maximize understanding between persons are effectively bracketed.

If it is appropriate to characterize the present era as an age of information, it is an open question what meaning such epistemic values as wisdom, practical judgment, and social criticism are capable of assuming within increasingly technological vocabularies. The knowledge-based society is certainly not one founded upon the several varieties of human knowing but upon varieties that are derivative from modern science alone. Ways of thinking or evaluating that can claim no such lineage are among those on which civility directly relies, and philosophers rightly worry when such values are relegated to the margins of social life. If technology has become the medium of social reality and the will to mastery belongs to technology's essence, privacy is not alone among values imperiled by its reign. Individual dignity, respect, and civility are values that resist incorporation into scientific, technological, or even utilitarian vocabularies. If the intelligence shall exist in the civilization now emerging that will effectively rein in the excesses of modern technology, it will be a kind of intelligence that is not itself technological.

PRINCIPLES

When small barriers of civility or respect come to be regarded within technological vocabularies as inefficiencies or anachronisms, their erosion is foreseeable. The ends that such barriers serve are not to make social relations efficient but to make them peaceful and free. The small scale of many privacy intrusions, and of the boundaries that they overstep, easily creates an appearance of insignificance, and insignificant they would perhaps remain were the problem not widespread and deeply rooted within the scientific-technological worldview. To speak of information privacy violations as a pervasive social ill—comparable in this respect to poverty, ignorance, or violence—may be dismissed as hyperbole, paranoia, or an affluent society's vexation. Yet to dismiss the matter as trifling overlooks the cumulative effect that information and surveillance technologies can exert on a culture and the dangerous consequences that can result when certain boundaries are systematically overstepped. Like power, privacy is an issue not only in instances of large-scale abuse but on the diminished scale of petty yet ubiquitous intrusions from which escape can be impossible.

If the issue of information privacy, then, is not a trifling one, neither is it one that will be resolved by technological means. The language of technology is one of efficiency and inefficiency, utility and disutility, while its limits are articulated within a family of ethical concepts that is qualitatively different. The latter is a vocabulary of public and private, of human rights and personal inviolability. Its central categories pertain not to instrumentality but to human agency and the normative structures that constitute its conditions of possibility. The right of privacy in particular affords the normative basis from which the question of data protection is appropriately regarded.

The premise of information privacy rights is that an individual retains presumptive ownership over information regarding one's person, that its circulation in public domains is accordingly a matter for which a person retains a broad latitude of choice. As Judith Wagner DeCew articulates it, "when technological advance clashes with privacy, it is imperative to seek a solution in which the technology does not dictate the extent of privacy protection, but instead the consumers and targeted individuals choose when and how much to protect or relinquish their privacy."[19] As a presumption, the right to information privacy does not require in the spirit of absolutism that no fact about a person (one's name, for instance) can be revealed without the person's consent but that the burden of justification lies with the agent of disclosure rather than its subject. Presumptively, personal information is the moral property of its subject rather than public property or the property of institutions.

Several principles of data protection stem from this premise. In related forms they have gained considerable legislative support in postindustrial societies generally over the past few decades and in combination give the right to information privacy practical significance. A representative articulation of these principles is found in the U.K. Data Protection Act of 1998. It requires that personal data

> 1. are processed fairly and lawfully
> 2. are only processed for one or more specified and lawful purposes; data cannot be used or disclosed for any purpose incompatible with the specified purposes for which it was collected, without the permission of the data subject
> 3. are adequate, relevant and not excessive for the purpose for which they are required
> 4. are accurate and up to date
> 5. are not kept any longer than is necessary for the purpose for which they are required
> 6. are processed in accordance with the rights of the data subject. . . . These include: the right to access any personal data held about them; to prevent processing of data that is likely to cause them damage or distress; and to prevent processing for the purpose of direct marketing
> 7. are protected from unauthorised or unlawful processing or loss
> 8. are not transferred to countries outside the European Union that do not have adequate data protection laws.[20]

As well as being representative of data protection measures that have taken hold in Europe and North America, these guidelines appropriately address a variety of issues brought about by contemporary information technologies. While principles alone do not resolve the difficult issue of enforcement, they afford the necessary ethical and legal framework in which information-based commerce and public services are appropriately governed. The central principles of information privacy include the idea that the intrusiveness of information requests from professionals or institutions ought to be the least necessary for the achievement of specific purposes, that data recorded in files be regularly updated or deleted if the purpose for which they were collected no longer exists, and that they not be sold or transferred to third parties without the subject's knowledge and consent. The existence of secret records is in no case justifiable; even in instances where security considerations require the classification of data or nonaccess by the subject of a file, the existence of such files ought not be a secret. Under normal circumstances persons are properly at liberty to inspect and correct inaccuracies within records that pertain to them, while access by others is appropriately limited to persons or agencies whose purpose in acquiring data is known to the subjects and not contradictory to their interests (exceptional cases being essentially law enforcement and national security matters).

As Colin Bennett notes, data protection legislation in various nations converges around principles of openness regarding the existence of personal records, access to and correction of such records, limits on data collection and third-party disclosure, limits on the uses to which data can be put (specifically, that information collected for one purpose cannot be used for another), and security provisions.[21] In each case the premise of data protection measures is that personal information circulated within public domains does not thereby cease to represent the moral property of the person to whom the information pertains. The challenge that information privacy continues to represent after a generation of legislation ultimately turns less on these principles than on enforcement issues and the reluctance of many (especially conservative) legislators to extend privacy protection to the private sector, wherein the problem is no less pressing than in public-sector institutions.

PRIVACY AND MEDICAL RECORDS

One area in which the issue of data protection is of particular sensitivity and importance is medical and psychiatric records, an issue that has become increasingly pressing since the advent of computerization and electronic files. The dilemma may be stated concisely: information regarding an individual's medical and/or psychiatric history must be readily available to medical professionals charged with his or her care, particularly in emergency situations, yet the ready availability of such information threatens a patient's privacy in potentially dangerous ways. The issue is not altogether new; in the days of paper records, privacy violations were hardly unknown. Files could easily fall into the wrong hands or be used for unethical purposes; however, computerization, modern information technology, and databases have dramatically altered the dimensions of the problem. To begin with, the sheer number of medical personnel to whom such information is available is now far larger than in the past. As one expert remarks,

> Dozens of health care workers have access to the typical hospitalized patient's health information. On a nursing unit, all nursing staff may have ready access to the information of all unit patients, whether or not they are caring for that patient. In a medical practice, all employees of the practice might have potential access to the information. Often, not all those who have potential access actually need that information. Unless an employee is involved in caring for a particular patient or in processing their health information (for example, for billing, transcription, or other business purposes), that employee should ordinarily not have access to the patient's record. . . . Even in computerized health information systems, the system's design sometimes does not bar unauthorized staff from accessing a particular patient's information. For example, unless the system has a way of recording who is "officially" involved in caring for the patient, it may be possible for any physician, nurse, laboratory technician, or other health care professional to look up any patient's information—even patients for whom that professional is not providing care.[22]

Recent estimates have it that in the United States 150 people on average will see a patient's medical file during a hospital visit.[23] Add to this the large number of researchers, administrators, policymakers, public health organizations, educators, and now (in this post–September 11 environment) intelligence agencies, all with "information needs" of one sort or another—not to mention computer "hackers"—and the scope of the problem is larger still. The sheer quantity of patient-specific information that is collected, stored, cross-referenced, and transferred with or without a patient's consent far exceeds what occurred in the time prior to electronic files or what ordinary reason would think necessary. One operative factor is that contemporary medical practice is a far cry from the days when one's physician and a handful of others possessed access to one's medical records and when such records took the form of paper files locked in filing cabinets. Today a hospital patient is veritably set upon by an array of professionals constituting what is called the "circle of care," a team of physicians, specialists, nurses, psychiatrists, psychologists, physiotherapists, pharmacists, technicians, clerks, and others, all of whose information needs are largely, if perhaps not always, legitimate. Facilitating communication between health care professionals and improving administrative efficiency are among the practical advantages that are made possible by information technology but are offset by increasing uncertainty regarding patient confidentiality.

The U.S. Patriot Act has added a further dimension to the issue; the law now permits FBI investigators to gain access to medical and many other personal files whenever the possibility of terrorism presents itself. The act, as one commentator notes, "permits FBI access to the books, documents, and records of *any* business (and apparently any non-business entity as well). As written, the new provision applies to employee and patient records as well as customer records; it applies to such businesses as credit-card companies, HMOs, magazine publishers, book sellers, and video rental stores; and it apparently reaches the files of such non-commercial entities as the Arab-American Anti-Defamation League, the Sierra Club, or any synagogue or mosque. And these amendments (like the amendments for financial records) drop the previous requirement that the records had to be those of a suspected foreign agent. Records pertaining to any American citizen now are available for FBI inspection on a clandestine basis whenever the agent states that the records 'are sought for an authorized investigation . . . to protect against international terrorism,' whether or not there is a basis for considering the targeted person a suspect or a foreign agent."[24]

As is so often the case in modern life, practical utilities may come into direct conflict with ethical considerations of a largely nonutilitarian or noninstrumental kind. Judging the relative importance of institutional efficiencies versus personal inviolability involves no simple tallying of utilities. No common measure underlies the various values that are at stake in such issues, making ethical vocabularies of instrumental rationality and utility largely irrelevant. Consider, for instance, the situation of the individual seeking either to purchase health or life insurance, apply for a job, or attend an educational institution and being required to answer invasive questions regarding one's medical and/or psychiatric history (or one's family's) and a wide assortment of lifestyle questions, often with little or no relevance to the application itself or none that is apparent to the individual him- or herself. That a student seeking an education or a person seeking employment should have to submit to a battery of questions, many highly personal and seemingly irrelevant, because of an institution's ostensible "information needs" would have been viewed as outrageous only a generation or two ago—when inquiring into one's personal income, for instance, was a veritable taboo—yet today it is a fact to which we have all become disturbingly accustomed. Practical dangers aside, the experience of vulnerability is that one never knows exactly how one's information will be framed, interpreted, and used; nor by whom or when; nor, in general, into what category of humanity one has been slotted and for what reason (aside from the fact that much of such information one may strongly prefer kept to oneself) it is a vulnerability to which the modern subject has become remarkably well adapted, perhaps to a fault. The practical dangers are formidable as well, ranging from persons avoiding medical treatment or withholding sensitive facts from health care professionals to companies making employment-related decisions on the basis of an individual's medical records. (One survey has it that 35 percent of American Fortune 500 companies have regarded health records as relevant factors in making employment decisions.[25]) Other examples familiar from common experience are so numerous that it is unnecessary to belabor the point: an individual's ability to acquire life or health insurance, to gain employment and career advancement, or even to attain an education or housing turns increasingly upon health information, which formerly was the moral property of the individual. Forms of discrimination—insurance, workplace, and otherwise—are virtual inevitabilities when persons are slotted into various types of "at risk" categories. Breaches of confidentiality within medical settings are hardly uncommon and can cause effects ranging from shame and embarrassment to more tangible harms. One survey indicates that as many as 24 percent of health professionals admitted to being "aware of violations of the confidentiality of individuals' medical records from inside an organization that embarrassed or harmed the individual."[26]

The question for legislators and jurists, of course, is how to protect personal data without undermining good medical practice as well as research and other public purposes. One eminently sensible proposal is M. Brandt's "least privilege" principle: that persons may be granted access to patient information only to the extent that is required for such persons to perform their professional roles.[27] In the case of public ends, the answer one most often hears today is that privacy must be "balanced" against competing social purposes, among which medical research is undoubtedly foremost. Researchers have long enjoyed access to such data with or without patients' knowledge or consent, on the grounds that such access is a necessary condition of the advancement of medical knowledge. Utilitarian justifications are readily available here, yet as is so often the case, when one set of values is "balanced" against a conflicting set, ostensibly for the betterment of all, one set tips the balance when conflicts arise. In the past, public purposes have tended to outweigh privacy, particularly where research is concerned. Although rarely stated explicitly, the background assumption is explicitly utilitarian: the public good, or any undertaking that purportedly serves it, trumps individuality and individual privacy. Taking privacy seriously requires questioning this assumption, well entrenched though it is within both ethical and legal frameworks. If we have good reason to regard privacy as a right, then, like other rights, it properly serves as a break on activities that require personal data for public ends. In the case of research, moreover, it is highly doubtful that data identifying patients by name is often a requirement of good research. No one doubts that studies require large quantities of data, yet that such data should be "identifying" (including names, addresses, and so on) is a distinct proposition and a dubious one in the vast majority of cases. In this day of advanced information technology it is not a difficult matter to delete identifying information from medical data to be used for research purposes or to substitute personal names with pseudonyms or codes. It would be difficult indeed to defend the claim that the dissemination of identifying information is normally, or perhaps ever, a vital requirement for research purposes unrelated to the direct care of a given patient.

Recognizing this, an increasing number of medical and industry associations, research councils, and government departments of health are urging that data intended for research and other secondary purposes be rendered anonymous wherever possible, although the policy is less frequently practiced than it might be. As Heidi Tranberg and Jem Rashbass note, "one of the factors contributing to this situation [of noncompliance] is the continuing uncertainty as to whether de-identification merely provides an additional level of privacy protection, or whether it can be used as a valid alternative to consent." They go on to propose that "in theory, there is no reason why anonymity should not be an alternative to consent, provided it is carried out effectively and consistently."[28] Much rides, of course, on the "in theory" proviso. The reality is that many medical, research, and other professionals who may be well familiar with the privacy policies that govern their respective institutions routinely fail to implement them for reasons of administrative efficiency or simple convenience. It is for this reason that de-identification is unlikely to replace or remove the need for consent and will remain but one strategy by which privacy may be safeguarded.

Improbable as well is the proposition that such information must be made available to researchers without patients' consent. While the question of consent would be moot should data destined for secondary purposes ever be rendered completely anonymous or pseudonymous, this happy eventuality is not likely to become a reality anytime soon. For as long as sensitive personal information remains the presumptive moral property of the patient rather than researchers or medical institutions, policymakers would be prudent to resist those speaking too quickly and carelessly of "the advancement of medical knowledge" where such advancement is alleged to require information that is often as unnecessary as it is invasive. Making an exception for cases in which "the public interest" ostensibly requires that data be transferred without patients' consent typically raises more difficulties than it resolves; laws, for instance, that provide for a public-interest exception to consent would need to be sufficiently general to capture a range of cases, and it is altogether impossible that a law could cast a net that effectively included all instances in which a reasonable person would agree that consent may be appropriately overridden without capturing too many other cases as well (unless such a law be limited to preventing identifiable harms to identifiable persons). The vagueness of the public-interest exception becomes dangerous when it is inevitably watered down and serves as an easy rationalization for privacy violations on the part of researchers and health professionals alike. To defend the consent requirement, of course, does not entail that in all cases such consent must be direct or express. In noncontentious cases, or when obtaining express consent is utterly impractical, implied consent will often suffice, provided that the transferring of data can be expected to benefit the patient in a significant way and that the patient could be expected with some reasonable probability to grant consent were he or she able.

Among the more effective recent legislative measures aimed at protecting medical information privacy is the Canadian province of Ontario's Personal Health Information Protection Act, which took effect in 2004. While similar in many ways to data protection laws in other North American and European jurisdictions, the act is among the more determined legislative attempts to negotiate the dilemma described here in ways that tip the balance in important ways toward privacy. Among other provisions, the bill requires patient consent for the collection and dissemination of personal health data; strengthens patients' rights to access records and correct errors; grants patients the right to instruct health care providers not to share information with other professionals; regulates the use of such information for research, marketing, and fund-raising purposes; grants patients the right to complain to Ontario's information and privacy commissioner in the event of a breach; and provides for legal remedies. Under the provisions of this law, "health care custodians" is a broad category including both individual professionals (physicians, nurses, psychologists, dentists, pharmacists) and institutions (hospitals, psychiatric facilities, laboratories, nursing homes, boards of health) who must, among other duties,

> obtain an individual's consent when collecting, using and disclosing personal health information . . . ; collect personal health information appropriately (by lawful means and for lawful purposes) and no more than is reasonably necessary; take reasonable precautions to safeguard personal health information even when it is used and disclosed outside of Ontario . . . ; ensure records are accurate, up-to-date and complete . . . ; ensure health records are stored, transferred and disposed of in a secure manner; inform an individual of any uses and dis-

> closures of personal health information without the individual's consent that occurred outside the custodian's information practices; [and] designate or take on the role of a contact person who is responsible for: responding to access/correction requests; responding to inquiries about the custodian's information practices; receiving complaints regarding any alleged breach of [this law].[29]

While the consent requirement specifies that patient consent be "knowledgeable" (meaning that "an individual must know why a health information custodian collects, uses or discloses his/her personal health information and that he/she may withhold or withdraw this consent"), such consent must be "express" rather than "implied" only in some cases, exceptions including the sharing of information with professionals within the patient's "circle of care" and the disclosure of names and addresses for fund-raising purposes. Express or direct consent is required in cases of disclosures to insurance companies and other organizations and persons outside the patient's circle of care, of disclosures between custodians for purposes other than providing health care, and of the collection or sharing of personal information for research purposes (with some qualifications) and marketing activities. As well, individuals may withdraw both express and implied consent to such disclosures at any time as well as place conditions on such consent both at the time that personal information is collected and at any time thereafter. Additional restrictions governing the collection of personal health data include the requirement that custodians collect information "directly from the individual involved and may only collect as much information as is necessary to meet the purpose of the collection," excepting circumstances where individuals consent to indirect collection when required or permitted by law, necessary for the provision of care and impossible to attain directly, required for management purposes, or when authorized directly by the information privacy commissioner. Health care custodians may disclose information without a patient's consent under specified conditions only, including

> if the disclosure is reasonably necessary for providing health care and the consent cannot be obtained in a timely manner, unless there is an express request from the individual instructing otherwise; for the purpose of contacting a relative or friend of an individual who is injured, incapacitated, ill or unable to give consent personally; to identify an individual who is deceased . . . ; to eliminate or reduce a significant risk of serious bodily harm to any person or the public; when transferring records to a custodian's successor or to the archives for conservation; for determining or verifying eligibility for publicly funded health care . . . ; for the purpose of legal proceedings [and] research,

. . . and a few others. This last condition is further qualified as follows: identifying data may be disseminated for medical research purposes without consent provided that researchers submit a detailed research plan to a research ethics board for approval, which will in turn require that "the research cannot be reasonably accomplished without access to information; there is a public interest in conducting the research; obtaining consent directly is impracticable; and adequate safeguards are in place to protect the privacy of individuals and the confidentiality of their information."[30] The law adds several further restrictions on researchers, including that they neither disclose identifying information nor publish data that could in any way identify individuals, that the use of information be solely for the purposes identified in the research plan, and compliance with any additional conditions imposed by the research ethics board. Finally, the new law establishes formal procedures by which patients can access their personal health information and correct errors, while also providing for administration and enforcement.

While the Ontario law goes as far or further than do many similar laws in other North American and European jurisdictions, its application remains limited to the public sector, leaving out some of the most important organizations and institutions that manage such information, including insurance companies, employers, and educational institutions. The Ontario law is typical in this respect, despite the fact that information privacy is no less an issue within the private sector than in public institutions and while no moral difference separates the question of information privacy in the two spheres. It would appear to be only the failure of political will and the hegemony of private-sector interests that limit the reach of this and similar laws to public-sector institutions. The rule within private institutions has long been that information privacy standards should be voluntary and self-imposed. The American Health Insurance Portability and Accountability Act of 1996, for example, applies only to medical records held by health care professionals, health plans, and health clearinghouses and even here only to records that are held and transmitted electronically; it does not apply to private employers, life insurance companies, or even public agencies that provide welfare and social security benefits. Under the act, government agencies, courts, insurance companies, the Medical Information Bureau, employers, and even direct marketers all enjoy ready access to medical records. If one expects to find an ethical rationale for this, one will be disappointed.

Critics of the public/private distinction seldom direct their critical efforts toward questions of information privacy or technologies of communication and surveillance, instead concentrating attention upon issues of property and domestic politics. Undoubtedly these represent two very different sets of issues, yet incommensurable they are not. The moral axis around which both revolve is the distinction between public and private. Its indispensability in confronting the problem of privacy in an information age ought to give us pause before jettisoning the distinction as an anachronism or a bulwark of ideology.

NOTES

1. See Paul Fairfield, *The Ways of Power: Hermeneutics, Ethics, and Social Criticism* (Pittsburgh, Pa.: Duquesne University Press, 2002), chap. 4.

2. Alan F. Westin, *Privacy and Freedom* (New York: Atheneum, 1967), 7.

3. David Lyon, "Surveillance as Social Sorting: Computer Codes and Mobile Bodies," in *Surveillance as Social Sorting: Privacy, Risk, and Digital Discrimination*, ed. David Lyon (New York: Routledge, 2003), 13.

4. Paul Sieghart, *Privacy and Computers* (London: Latimer, 1976), 75–76.

5. David F. Linowes, *Privacy in America* (Chicago: University of Illinois Press, 1989), 160.

6. Peter Shane, John Podesta, and Richard Leone, eds., introduction to *A Little Knowledge: Privacy, Security, and Public Information After September 11* (New York: Century Foundation Press, 2004), 8.

7. Martin Heidegger, "The Question Concerning Technology," in *Basic Writings*, ed. David Krell, trans. W. Lovitt (New York: Harper and Row, 1977), 289, 299.

8. Deckle McLean, *Privacy and Its Invasion* (Westport, Conn.: Praeger, 1995), 117.

9. As one organization devoted to electronic privacy observes, "the implications [of the Patriot Act] for online privacy are considerable. For example, it increases the ability of law enforcement agencies to authorize installation of pen registers and trap and trace devices (a pen register collects the outgoing phone numbers placed from a specific telephone line; a trap and trace device captures the incoming numbers placed to a specific phone line—a caller-id box is a trap and trace device), and to authorize the installation of such devices to record all computer routing, addressing, and signaling information. The Act also extends the government's ability to gain access to personal financial information and student information without any suspicion of wrongdoing, simply by certifying that the information likely to be obtained is relevant to an ongoing criminal investigation." Electronic Privacy Information Center, "The USA Patriot Act," www.epic.org/privacy/terrorism/usapatriot/default/html (accessed June 6, 2005), 6.

10. Amitai Etzioni, "Introduction: Rights and Responsibilities, Post 9/11," *Rights vs. Public Safety After 9/11: America in the Age of Terrorism*, eds. Amitai Etzioni and Jason H. Marsh (Lanham, Md.: Rowman & Littlefield, 2003), ix–x.

11. Richard Posner, "The Truth About Our Liberties," in Etzioni and Marsh, *Rights vs. Public Safety*, 26, 27.

12. One organization that has resisted the trend is the American Civil Liberties Union, which has rightfully complained of the innumerable abuses that the Patriot Act has made possible: "we are in danger of allowing ourselves to be governed by our fears, rather than our values. How else can we explain the actions of our government

over the last two years to invade the privacy of our personal lives and to curtail immigrants' rights, all in the name of increasing our security?" "ACLU Testimony at a Hearing on 'America After 9/11: Freedom Preserved or Freedom Lost?' before the Senate Judiciary Committee, Submitted by Nadine Strossen and Timothy Edgar, November 18, 2003," www.aclu.org/safeandfree/safeandfree.cfm (accessed July 21, 2005). Along similar lines, David Cole has argued, "Three principles in particular should guide our response to the threat of terrorism. First, we should not overreact in a time of fear, a mistake we have made all too often in the past. Second, we should not sacrifice the bedrock foundations of our constitutional democracy—political freedom and equal treatment—absent a compelling showing of need and adoption of narrowly tailored means. And third, in balancing liberty and security, we should not succumb to the temptation to trade a vulnerable minority's liberties, namely, the liberties of immigrants in general or Arab and Muslim immigrants in particular, for the security of the rest of us. Unfortunately, the USA Patriot Act, our government's first legislative attempt to respond to the threats posed by September 11, violates all three of these principles." "Let's Fight Terrorism, Not the Constitution," in Etzioni and Marsh, *Rights vs. Public Safety*, 35. Stephen Schulhofer offers the eminently sensible view that "nothing could be more foreign to American democracy, or more dangerous, than the assumption that in a time of crisis, scrutiny and criticism of governmental action are unnecessary, unpatriotic, or obstructionist. No features of our political structure are more central and important than our commitments to separation of powers, checks and balances, and the maximum feasible degree of public discussion and debate—even in wartime." Schulhofer, *The Enemy Within: Intelligence Gathering, Law Enforcement, and Civil Liberties in the Wake of September 11* (New York: Century Foundation Press, 2002), 2.

13. Michel Foucault, *Discipline and Punish: The Birth of the Prison*, trans. Alan Sheridan (New York: Vintage Books, 1979), 202–3.

14. Jeffrey Reiman, *Critical Moral Liberalism: Theory and Practice* (Lanham, Md.: Rowman & Littlefield, 1997), 175.

15. Reiman, *Critical Moral Liberalism*, 182.

16. See especially Martin Heidegger, "The Question Concerning Technology" and "The Age of the World Picture," in *The Question Concerning Technology and Other Essays*, trans. W. Lovitt (New York: Harper Colophon Books, 1977).

17. Investigative resources are widely available, for instance, on Internet sites that for a small fee provide access to a variety of electronic records. Marketed to the general public, such sites promise to "locate long lost friends, relatives, a past lover who broke your heart," "learn all about your mysterious neighbors," "discover dirty secrets your in-laws don't want you to know," or "learn how to get information on an ex-spouse that will help you win in court."

18. Irma van der Ploeg, "Biometrics and the Body as Information: Normative Issues of the Socio-technical Coding of the Body," in Lyon, *Surveillance as Social Sorting*, 58–59.

19. Judith Wagner DeCew, *In Pursuit of Privacy: Law, Ethics, and the Rise of Technology* (Ithaca, N.Y.: Cornell University Press, 1997), 161.

20. Heidi Tranberg and Jem Rashbass, *Medical Records: Use and Abuse* (Oxford: Radcliffe Medical Press, 2004), 9.

21. Colin J. Bennett, *Regulating Privacy: Data Protection and Public Policy in Europe and the United States* (Ithaca, N.Y.: Cornell University Press, 1992), 101–11.

22. Jill Callahan Dennis, *Privacy and Confidentiality of Health Information* (San Francisco: Jossey-Bass, 2000), 4–5.

23. S. George, "Medical Privacy and Medical Research," *Newsletter of the Cancer and Leukemia Society B* 11 (2002): 2.

24. Schulhofer, *Enemy Within*, 51.

25. D. Linowes, "Research Survey of Privacy in the Workplace," unpublished paper, University of Illinois, Urbana-Champaign, 1997.

26. *Harris-Equifax Consumer Privacy Survey* (Atlanta, Ga.: Equifax, 1993).

27. M. Brandt, *Information Security: An Overview* (Chicago: American Health Information Management Association, 1996).

28. Tranberg and Rashbass, *Medical Records*, 145.

29. Information and Privacy Commission, *Frequently Asked Questions: Personal Health and Information Protection Act* (Toronto, Ontario: Information and Privacy Commission), 12, www.ipc.on.ca/docs/hfaq-e.pdf (accessed July 31, 2005). See also "Personal Health Information Protection Act, 2004," www.e-laws.gov.on.ca/DBLaws/Statutes/English/04p03_e.htm (accessed July 21, 2005).

30. Information and Privacy Commission, *Frequently Asked Questions*, 24–27.

Chapter Three

Political Philosophy in the Bedroom

POLITICAL MORALISM

When former Canadian prime minister Pierre Elliott Trudeau declared in 1969 that "the state has no place in the bedrooms of the nation," he was signaling a fundamental departure from the political morality of his own and of virtually all prior times.[1] A student of liberalism, Trudeau would qualify this statement in two important respects: "so long as what's done hurts nobody and is done between consenting adults."[2] On the face of it, this statement sounds like textbook liberalism, yet it is one likely to find support as well among many social democrats, feminists, proponents of lesbian and gay rights, and others. The sentiment that it expresses draws upon the distinction between public and private while deploying the distinction in an area of public policy that had hitherto been the preserve of conservatism—the domain of marriage, family life, and sexual morality. The context that provoked Trudeau's remark was a general debate in Canada, as in many other countries at the time, that led to the decriminalization of homosexual activity and a loosening of restrictions on divorce and abortion. Such legislative reform had aroused no little controversy, as it continues to do among conservatives today, particularly among the religiously oriented and particularly in the United States.

These applications of the right to privacy at long last called into question the hegemony of what one might call *political moralism*, a philosophy of ancient lineage that advocates the inscription in law of the standards of morality professed by a majority in a given state. While no society is without a conception of political morality, what I am calling political moralism stems more particularly from the premise that there is no principled limit upon the power of a majority to fashion as law a particular conception of virtue or that majority decision alone constitutes that limit. Among political conservatives, the definition of *virtue* is thought largely to go without saying, with the only persons likely to dissent being the morally unsound. Such conservatives traditionally defend a conception of the private as it applies to property and market relations but not in areas of moral conduct, most especially sexuality. The latter areas not only fall squarely within the public domain, such conservatives hold, but are enjoined by moral standards upheld by all right-thinking persons and backed by the force of law. A generation after Trudeau's remark, and after similar legislative reform in many other nations, the forces of political conservatism have not only reasserted themselves but redrawn the axes around which much political debate revolves; morality politics would displace the "liberalism" of the 1960s and 1970s, a reaction to what are often viewed as the moral excesses of the time. Individual privacy is among the casualties of conservative politics, along with other rights that appear to intimate moral laxity.

The basic question at the heart of this debate might be articulated as follows: What precisely is the role of the state in regulating sexual morality and family life? More specifically, are acts committed by consenting adults which violate no rights yet which are deemed distasteful or morally unacceptable by a majority (so-called victimless crimes) legitimate objects of legal proscription? The social conservative's affirmative reply rests squarely on the assumption that intimate relations fall within the public domain. On the face of it, there is something deeply counterintuitive in the conservative position: intimate relations, we are accustomed to thinking, are private by their very nature. Romantic lovers must regularly retreat from the public gaze, limit public displays of affection, and so on, suggesting that intimacy belongs necessarily to the sphere of private life. Yet at the same time, social conservatives would legislate against sexual practices that a majority or tradition deems immoral. Such acts as adultery, fornication, and sodomy (to use some antiquated expressions) continue to be criminal offenses in many states, although enforcement of such laws is typically lax. Where such laws remain on the books, their primary purpose is to make statements concerning the values of the majority rather than to serve the usual function of law. Those on the other side of the political fence doubt either that they are statements worth making or that it is a legitimate function of public institutions to make statements of any kind regarding private matters, no matter how widely shared such sentiments are.

While in certain cases it appears that what is at stake in such debates is symbolism alone, often the stakes are far higher, as the abortion issue demonstrates and as is illustrated as well in antidiscrimination law, where rights of gays and lesbians concerning adoption, child custody, military service, professional employment, and so on, come directly into play. Laws that bear upon sexual orientation and discrimination are far from mere symbolism, as is the issue of same-sex marriage, which has aroused much, and bitter, controversy of late.

At present, political moralism finds rather broad favor among legislators and activists, not all of whom are conservative. In the United States many Republicans adopt this view, inspired by an enthusiasm for the traditional conception of the family along with an antipathy toward abortion, divorce, homosexuality, and so on. Conservative parties and organizations in many other democratic societies are similarly inspired, while more liberal legislators as well often subscribe to their own variants of political moralism. Among political theorists of the present day, proponents of this view are decidedly fewer in number than those among their activist counterparts. While some proponents of communitarianism approach the political philosophy of which I am speaking, one finds perhaps the clearest statement of defense of this position in Patrick Devlin's *The Enforcement of Morals*, a book written in the 1960s in response to the Wolfenden report that had been commissioned by the British government in 1957 and whose task it was to provide recommendations to the government on the subjects of homosexuality and prostitution and the laws that pertain to them.

In this book Devlin argues without reservation that the moral values of a majority of citizens in a given state are the sole legitimate basis of law and that in principle there is no constraint upon a democratic majority that wishes to enforce its conception of virtue and the good life by legislative means. As Devlin asserts,

> It is wrong to talk of private morality or of the law not being concerned with immorality as such or to try to set rigid bounds to the part which the law may play in the suppression of vice. There are no theoretical limits to the power of the State to legislate against treason and sedition, and likewise I think there can be no theoretical limits to legislation against immorality.[3]

As for what constitutes immorality, "society" is thought by Devlin to have little difficulty in identifying this; legislators must look to the "community of ideas"—political, ethical, and religious—that affords the normative standards of a society. Foreshadowing communitarianism, Devlin writes,

> Society means a community of ideas; without shared ideas on politics, morals, and ethics no society can exist. Each one of us has ideas about what is good and what is evil; they cannot be kept private from the society in which we live. If men and women try to create a society in which there is no fundamental agreement about good and evil they will fail; if, having based it on common agreement, the agreement goes, the society will disintegrate. For society is not something

> that is kept together physically; it is held by the invisible bonds of common thought. If the bonds were too far relaxed the members would drift apart. A common morality is part of the bondage. The bondage is part of the price of society; and mankind, which needs society, must pay its price.[4]

Devlin mentions as examples of moral beliefs that comprise this "fundamental agreement" the traditional Christian conception of marriage and the intolerance of homosexuality.[5] If Christian morality is fundamental to the political or general culture of a given state, then non-Christians, gays, lesbians, and others not a party to the prevailing community of ideas can be expected both to comply with democratic law and to acknowledge the necessity of doing so. The common abhorrence of gays and lesbians that Devlin notes legitimates legal proscription of their conduct provided that such disgust "is deeply felt and not manufactured."[6]

To more contemporary readers these are harsh statements indeed. Within scholarly circles they are anything but orthodox at the present time, yet the sentiments that they express continue to underlie many contemporary laws, legislative programs, political platforms, and activist organizations. The rough edges of this general view are typically smoothed over by their more diplomatic proponents, yet in its essentials political moralism remains a major force in contemporary political affairs. It is a view defended more recently by Richard Posner and Michael Levin in the context of discussions of sexual morality and the law.[7] Posner, for instance, argues in *Sex and Reason* not only that moral feelings afford the proper basis of law but that such feelings—including intolerance of homosexuality—are "datum" for moral and political reasoning, quite beyond the reach of social criticism: "If prostitution, homosexuality, fornication, or any other offense against traditional Christian sexual morality evoked as wide and deep an antipathy as infanticide, gladiatorial contests, or suicide, those offenses would *be* immoral. Period. There would be no purchase for critique."[8] "Strong emotions," Posner writes (among which he includes disgust), "in fact supply the sturdiest foundations for moral feelings"[9] and hence for law as well. Recent communitarian scholars as well often defend (or appear to defend) a kinder, gentler version of Devlin's view, but even here the major portion of communitarian argumentation continues to take the form of criticism of opposed positions (chiefly liberal individualism) rather than an affirmation of an identifiable program. Michael Sandel, to take one example, repeats often what he takes to be the untenable philosophical assumptions of political liberalism and of many judicial rulings and legislative measures stemming from it, yet he offers the most ambiguous statement of the alternative he favors.[10] As with much of the communitarian literature, we find dismay over the crass excesses of "rights talk" intertwined with favorable references to community, the common good, virtue, family, and so on. Yet what we seldom find are clear affirmations of alternatives. Whether the explanation for this lies in the uncomfortable similarities between communitarian politics and Devlin's unambiguous and unapologetic view, one is left to ponder.

Communitarians and conservatives, however, are not alone in maintaining that law is properly based on the moral convictions of citizens; in their own ways liberals, social democrats, feminists, and others often premise their own political programs on moral commitments of one kind or another. Political moralism assumes a variety of forms and, when appropriately qualified, admits of far less controversy than when stated boldly. It is in the qualifications that the real issue lies, including the place of individual rights in limiting the power of communities or (more accurately) majorities in legislating for a particular conception of virtue or against what they deem to be vicious. Where the politics of the bedroom is concerned, however, it is the forces of social conservatism that often carry the most influence, particularly where such conservatism assumes religious form. Within constitutional democracies of the present day, Christian conservatism undoubtedly is not the force that it once was. For generations this view depended for its credibility upon a broad-based and largely tacit consensus regarding sexual and other ethical matters, a consensus that has been slowly eroded by the rise of pluralism and a host of related factors. Indeed in many nations Christian conservatism has declined so radically that political observers from those nations look with some dismay upon developments over the past few decades in the one country in which conservatism in this form has alone rebounded.

The United States of America has from its inception been indelibly marked by the Puritanism of many of its founders. While the democratic nations of Europe and elsewhere have tended to incorporate a degree of liberality in law bearing upon homosexuality, divorce, abortion, and so on, American legislators by and large have been slow to follow their lead. At a time when Christian theology is not regarded as a credible force in mainstream politics in many other democratic societies, many to all American states continue to legislate against fornication, adultery, prostitution, sodomy, and same-sex marriage. Legal discrimination and harassment of gays and lesbians remain commonplace, and while America continues to regard itself as a nation of equality and tolerance, its native and somewhat aggressive religiosity limits such values, sometimes to the vanishing point. A comparison with its neighbor to the north reveals a profound difference in the influence of Christian conservatism in American and Canadian political cultures. There is in Canada nothing to compare with the religious right of the United States in terms of political influence; conservative politicians and organizations in Canada typically must soft-pedal their own religiosity in order to achieve mainstream respectability, as do Christian politicians of other parties. American law, by contrast, has always reflected the ebb and flow of evangelicalism and nowhere more so than in the province of human sexuality. There has long been in the United States, as many who are not American have observed, a general atmosphere of embarrassment and moral unease surrounding sexuality that is oddly comingled with an imperative to speak of it tirelessly. It is doubtful, for example, that a "sex scandal" as pedestrian as the one that set America astir for a prolonged period during the Clinton years would have had a comparable effect in virtually any other democratic society. This moral unease is directly reflected in American law, which both criminalizes more varieties of sexual conduct than do other democratic societies and punishes sexual immorality on the whole with greater severity than do those societies. This tendency within American political culture is closely related to an ambivalent paternalism that by turns proclaims the liberty of the individual while insisting that the community or tradition really knows what is best.

On the particular subject of sexual orientation, however, America is hardly alone in tending to regard homosexuality in a morally dim light and in upholding laws that reflect this. No matter what gains the principles of tolerance and equality appear to have made over the past generation or so—evidenced by the thorough disrepute of sexism, racism, and so on—intolerance of gays and lesbians continues to receive the qualified support of common morality. While for a growing number this attitude of disdain or "homophobia" appears as bigotry's last stand, conventional morality continues to give this sentiment a kind of limited blessing. To explain why this is so calls upon the efforts of the psychologist no less than the moralist, yet I limit my focus for the time being to the moral arguments that support the propositions that homosexuality is morally debased and an appropriate object of public concern.

While the latter proposition stands or falls on the premise of political moralism—on the view, that is, that what is distasteful or unacceptable to the majority is by that fact alone a public matter—arguments for the immorality of homosexuality are of similarly ancient origin. In the Western world, it is within the tradition of Judeo-Christian morality that one finds support for antipathy toward homosexuality, particularly toward gay men. Although the Bible itself makes only passing references to the subject relative to other acts it deems evil, the movement that it inspired has for centuries reserved some of its harshest sentiments for gays and lesbians.[11] The view of Pope Benedict XVI, for example—that while being gay is not in itself a sin, its expression in sexual acts is—is characteristic of many Christian sentiments. Its scriptural basis is found essentially in Leviticus and the Letters of Paul, although in the former the context in which homosexuality is designated an "abomination" bears not on matters of sexual morality but on rules of diet. Curiously, while "abomination" belongs among the strongest terms of biblical condemnation, it is a term applied as well in Leviticus and elsewhere to the eating of pork and shellfish, as well as to the act of wearing clothing of persons of the opposite gender. By contrast, scarcely a book of the Bible fails to condemn in the gravest terms such vices as adultery, irreligion, or lying—sins that arouse a fraction of the animosity that religious conservatives typically direct toward gays. As Laurence Thomas remarks,

> If one were to go by the amount of attention that contemporary evangelists and religious leaders devote to the topic of homosexuality, one would surely be warranted in concluding that according to the Bible homosexual behavior, perhaps more than any other behavior, is what has stood in the way of the righteous perfection of humankind. One might even be convinced that the sin of homosexuality is one of the major themes of the biblical text.[12]

The writings of Paul as well have frequently inspired jurists and persons generally to look upon gays and lesbians with disdain or legitimated such a tendency among legislators, raising the question whether the same writings would properly inspire laws or judicial rulings concerning women, given the quantity of opinions that Paul expressed on the subject.

Moral and political arguments that have their basis in scriptural authority are not ones that modern philosophers have tended to regard with great seriousness, even as their influence among politicians, courts, activists, and the general public continues to be great.[13] Not only in America is homosexuality commonly regarded as being morally dubious, and if this sentiment is often more aggressively asserted there than it is in many other nations, its effects are nonetheless felt in laws and attitudes throughout the world. The religious mind invariably posits an "other," normally a demonized other, against which it fashions its own self-understanding. The Evil One of Christian theology is a notable case in point, as is the figure of the depraved homosexual cast in the mythical role of the unsaved, without whom there could be none who are saved. It appears a universal feature of religious logic that the enlightened or chosen ones are very far from comprising the entire human race but are limited to those special persons who share the way of being of one's group. It is unsurprising that gays, having never constituted a majority in any culture of which we know, have tended to be regarded in history with disapprobation by heterosexual majorities and that religion has been called upon to sanctify the sexual orientation of majorities and to discredit all others.

An argument closely related to the appeal to religious authority is that which appeals to "nature" or to a conception of what is "natural." In common parlance this frequently encountered argument turns upon the hypothesis that homosexuality runs counter to what is somewhat ambiguously termed *nature* or *human nature*, although it is an argument that typically reduces to simple assertion and counterassertion. The hypothesis that homosexuality is in some sense unnatural is often theologically tinged, yet it also finds expression in secular language. In theological form the argument essentially restates the appeal to religion in a slightly altered fashion, while in its more secular, "scientific" form an appeal is made to the biological functioning of the human organism and its assorted parts. On the latter view, sexual practices that are unrelated to procreation are unnatural. With the biological purpose of sex being the reproduction of the species, any acts that are not conducive to this end represent misuses of the sexual organs. Every organ in the human body, in this scheme of things, has a specialized function designed by nature or God; employing that organ for a purpose other than that for which nature designed it negates its purpose and is accordingly unnatural and perverse. Michael Levin, defending this view, writes, "this is why homosexuality is abnormal, why male homosexuals are misusing their penises and lesbians their labia: their systematically nonfunctional use of their genitals has usurped their genitals' proper sexual role."[14] Perversity or unnaturalness is defined by Levin as "displacement of function,"[15] a view defended as well by Elizabeth Anscombe and Sara Ruddick.[16] Each of these authors articulates the frequently encountered view of homosexual acts as being debased (or, as Ruddick prefers, "incomplete") in view of their dissociation from reproduction, a dissociation that, according to Levin, "helps explain the antipathy toward [homosexuality]."[17]

As one might expect, this argument is taken with about as much seriousness by philosophers of the present day as the first argument, even as it retains a powerful hold on the consciousness of the general public and persons elected to public office. To many, "unnatural" seems a more legitimate epithet of condemnation than does "repellent" or "unsettling," having as it does an ethical connotation absent from the latter terms—although the latter do likely express more accurately the emotional reaction of many to the phenomenon of which I am speaking. It is a concept formerly employed in popular debates regarding contraception and abortion, among other things, and enjoys a long history of use within Catholic doctrine in particular. Ultimately, of course, its roots may be traced to ancient Greek philosophy, most especially to Plato, who appears to have been the first thinker in the Western tradition to speak of homosexuality as being biologically unnatural.[18] If animals in nature did not engage in homosexual activity, Plato reasoned, surely rational beings must refrain as well. With the subordination of appetite to reason being fundamental to the Platonic conception of human nature, it is no less fundamental to ethics and politics wherein human reason is brought to bear on practical affairs. While Plato's view does not appear to have significantly affected Greek or Roman civilization—evidenced by the relative tolerance in both societies for homosexuality, including legal tolerance—it readily found a home in Christian thought, where it remains influential to this day.

Appeals to nature, however, or natural law in the philosophy of human sexuality are not limited to the Platonic and Judeo-Christian traditions. The same appeal is made in the libertine tradition in efforts to redeem sexual practices of any and all varieties, be they heterosexual or homosexual. Here as well the natural, or the biological, is the ground of sexual morality. The writings of the Marquis de Sade, for instance, are rich in references to nature and natural law: "nature wills it; for a bridle have nothing but your inclinations, for laws your desires, for morality Nature's alone."[19] De Sade, of course, provides a very different reading of nature's law than the one passed down to us through tradition. Which of these readings more accurately represents nature's own text is not a matter I propose to resolve.

The difficulties with this course of argument, of course, are myriad and almost too obvious to state. Were it not for its considerable hold upon common opinion, one would be within one's rights in dismissing it out of hand. I limit myself to identifying several assumptions necessary to the conclusion that "unnatural" acts are properly proscribed by law. The argument in its platonic formulation assumes that homosexual acts are not to be found in the animal world (an empirically false claim), while in all formulations it assumes, among other things, that nature or human nature is an altogether given matter, that homosexuality is antireproductive, that the human significance of sexuality is defined strictly by reproduction, that every organ of the human body possesses a single natural function, that nature is ontologically prior to culture, that nature provides a metaphysical foundation for morality, and that what is immoral should therefore be illegal. These assumptions range in truth value from the eminently questionable to the evidently false.

The category of the "natural," of course, where human action is concerned signifies only the familiar, the majoritarian, or the culturally habitual. It comprises the sum of human acts that by virtue of their being common have taken on an appearance of necessity, an observation that John Stuart Mill made as far back as 1869: "So true is it," he wrote, "that unnatural generally means only uncustomary, and that everything which is usual appears natural."[20] It would appear to be a common feature of human consciousness that the familiar regularly becomes transformed into the necessary or the natural. As ideas recede to the background of the understanding, their contingency is forgotten; they are transformed into matters of a priori necessity, deviations from which demand an accounting or, in the case of human action, moral justification.

A similar logic is at work in the distinction often drawn between the normal and the deviant, a dichotomy regularly appealed to in discussions of sexual orientation. This scientific-sounding distinction ostensibly incorporates neither theological nor ethical assumptions in a way that the natural/unnatural distinction evidently does. Unlike the unnatural, the deviant is defined solely with reference to normal—in the sense of majority-sanctioned—standards of conduct, without the necessary implication of immorality. In principle at least, deviant acts need not be unethical. They are, however, perverse, and in a sense that is far from admitting a positive or even neutral connotation. Thus Sara Ruddick speaks of homosexuality as deviant or perverse while resisting the judgment of immorality. More boldly, Michael Levin characterizes it as unethical, unnatural, and deviant. "Homosexuality," according to Levin, "is a dysfunction, as counterselective a trait as is imaginable."[21] Roger Scruton draws a similar conclusion while attempting to identify precisely in what such dysfunction consists. He writes, "In the heterosexual act, it might be said, I move out *from* my body *towards* the other, whose flesh is unknown to me; while in the homosexual act I remain locked within my body, narcissistically contemplating in the other an excitement that is the mirror of my own."[22] Scruton's rather a priori analysis of same-sex intimacy characterizes it as being invariably deviant on account of its departure from sexual normalcy. Normal sexuality, Scruton maintains, includes an overcoming of psychosexual distance between persons; when the persons in question are of the same gender, such distance is reduced to a point of quasi narcissism, closer in kind to autoeroticism than intimacy. Levin carries this analysis to its logical conclusion: "It is questionable, in my view, whether [homosexuals] ever experience the emotion of love, as opposed to lust, infatuation, and other drives also familiar to heterosexuals."[23]

The division of sexual orientations and acts into normal and deviant, as Michel Foucault has remarked, has its roots in nineteenth-century psychology and medicine. At that time the "homosexual," as a distinct sexual type, was born together with the pedophile, the transvestite, the sadist, the masochist, and so on. The age of science gave rise to the practice of dividing social phenomena in general into discrete categories, causes of which were sought—particularly in instances of deviance—labels assigned, diagnoses pronounced, and so on. No longer a dimension of normal (if forbidden) sexuality, "homosexuality" was now a human type.

> The nineteenth-century homosexual became a personage, a past, a case history, and a childhood, in addition to being a type of life, a life form, and a morphology, with an indiscreet anatomy and possibly a mysterious physiology. Nothing that went into his total composure was unaffected by his sexuality. It was everywhere present in him: at the root of all his actions because it was their insidious and indefinitely active principle; written immodestly on his face and body because it was a secret that always gave itself away. It was consubstantial with him, less as a habitual sin than as a singular nature. . . . Homosexuality appeared

> as one of the forms of sexuality when it was transposed from the practice of sodomy onto a kind of interior androgyny, a hermaphrodism of the soul. The sodomite had been a temporary aberration; the homosexual was now a species.[24]

Twentieth-century psychology, particularly psychoanalysis, would often speak of homosexuality in medical terms as a sickness rooted in infantile conflicts imperfectly resolved. For Freud and many who followed him, infantile psychosexual development passed in the normal course of things through stages that culminated in adult heterosexuality, departures from which constitute unsatisfactory resolutions to instinctual conflicts of childhood. While Freud fully realized the extent to which latent homosexual drives remained a part of the psychosexual life of the adult throughout life, this particular view found less popular favor than the psychologization and medicalization of homosexuality or its transformation in scientific and popular consciousness to a dimension of deviant psychology—a transformation that seemed to cohere with judgments of unnaturalness and immorality. The assimilation of homosexuality to mental illness survived in the public mind the decision of the American Psychiatric Association in 1973 to remove it from the catalog of mental disorders.

Among the several sexual orientations of which we know, little light is cast in separating these into normal and deviant. It is eminently doubtful that in the domain of human sexuality—surely one of the most complex and subterranean of phenomena—there exists a unified and monolithic mode of orientation or behavior that may be identified without further ado as being normal, from which any and all departures fall into the category of deviance. From an ethical standpoint the distinction serves even less purpose, its true intention being merely to sanctify the sexual habits of majorities and to castigate the rest. The designation of normality, here as elsewhere, provides reassurance that all is as it should be, that no matter what frustration one may be experiencing, such frustration is normal—that is, unproblematic—or that, at any rate, it is less problematic than that of certain types of persons. What ought to give us pause in all of this is not the refusal of contemporary psychology to deem gays and lesbians deviant but the investment that so many have in regarding themselves and their sexuality as normal.

Other arguments have been advanced for the immorality of homosexuals and the necessity of relegating such persons by legal means to the margins of social life. What all such arguments have in common, be they ancient or modern, is a certain disingenuousness which becomes immediately evident upon inspection of the arguments themselves and the psychological note on which they are asserted. Merely to render such arguments explicit is to perceive them for what they are: rationalizations of raw animosity. Opposition to gay liberation, or to gays period, commonly appeals to vocabularies of moral disapprobation and "science" to lend legitimacy to the mixture of revulsion and fear that is its source. Whatever the psychological forces in play—and there is more in this of psychology than of morality—the critic of homosexuality mistakes plain revulsion for moral disapproval.

It ought to go without saying—and to a growing number it does—that there is nothing whatever that is unethical about homosexuality, whether as an orientation or in its forms of expression. This statement is as axiomatic as that different races, genders, and nationalities are morally equal, irrespective of the centuries of prejudice that weigh against each of these statements. Already in the eighteenth century, when ethical theorists were gradually severing ties with theology, Jeremy Bentham pronounced the conclusion not only of utilitarianism but of secular morality in general on the subject of homosexuality:

> To what class of offences shall we refer these irregularities of the venereal appetite which are styled unnatural? . . . I have been tormenting myself for years to find if possible a sufficient ground for treating them with the severity with which they are treated at this time of day by all European nations: but upon the principle of utility I can find none.[25]

Once the theological underpinnings of morality had been removed, no credible basis remained for the received view of homosexuality. As ethics came to bear more directly upon human happiness and freedom, the implication for the issue of sexual orientation was clear: "As to any primary mischief, it is evident that [homosexual activity] produces no pain in anyone. On the contrary it produces pleasure, and that a pleasure which, by their perverted taste, is by this supposition preferred to that pleasure which is in general reputed the greatest."[26] The lone qualification Bentham would add to this statement is that such acts—as with practices in general—must cause no harm to the parties involved.

Yet even if Bentham's conclusion is refused, it does not follow that if homosexuality is somehow morally tainted, it is for that reason legitimate for public institutions to tolerate discrimination or to proscribe conduct of gays and lesbians that causes no harm. The doctrine of political moralism fails for several reasons, a few of which H. L. A. Hart identified in his reply to Patrick Devlin,[27] as well as for reasons familiar to students of liberalism. As Hart and other liberal theorists maintain, there is a domain of private conduct that is outside the legitimate reach of legislation. While Hart regards the basic purpose of law as the maximization of welfare, liberals also regard the maximization of freedom and social peace as being fundamental to law and to public institutions generally. In either case, it is not the purpose of legislators to inscribe into law any and all moral sentiments that are widely shared in a society. Doing so potentially diminishes autonomy in the extreme. It is a society not of virtue but of conformity that is entailed most obviously in Devlin's unqualified conception of political moralism and more subtly by communitarian interpretations of the same doctrine.

In a free society individuals are at liberty to avoid social contact with gays or lesbians just as they are free to shun persons of other races or religions against whom they may harbor ill will. What they are not able to do is fashion their animosity as law or otherwise import such sentiments into the public domain in ways that diminish the rights of minorities. Any number of utilitarian arguments may be offered in support of this statement (including the deleterious effects of unenforced or unenforcible law, the likelihood of undesirable police and prosecutorial practices, a declining respect for law, and a conformist society); however, it is the principles of privacy and equal freedom that provide the appropriate philosophical basis for this view.

Old arguments for religious tolerance arising from the religious wars of early modern Europe have as their contemporary counterpart the general debate surrounding sexual orientation and law, and it may be hoped that the resolution to the latter debate will parallel the former. In order for this to occur we shall need to examine closely the relations between the issue before us, private religiosity, and the imperative of toleration.

PRIVACY AND INTIMATE RELATIONS

From the point of view of the Christian in a predominantly Christian society (or a Muslim in an Islamic society), for what reason ought one not support legislative measures that would effectively Christianize the society? It is not any lack of confidence in the truth of one's creed that generates respect for religious freedom; on the contrary, one will frequently harbor the deepest conviction that nonbelievers or persons of other faiths are both ignorant of the truth and morally wayward. One may even be right about this. The religious majority may practice their virtues in a manner entirely above reproach while others languish in the depths of iniquity. And yet the idea persists in many religious societies that the spiritual is a private matter, that religious minorities and nonbelievers are free to follow their own paths, and that church and state are separate realms. From a historical point of view, the principles of religious freedom and tolerance emerged out of generations of conflict and constituted a kind of truce to which rival sects could agree. The same principles also gave expression to a different idea, however, which was that religiosity does not belong within the province of politics or law, that the realm of the spiritual issued imperatives all its own which behooved the faithful but not all persons in the society. Religiosity that inscribed itself in law crossed a line, effectively removing it from the realm of the sacred and the personal to that of the compulsory and the public. There is a sense in which spirituality negated itself in departing that from which it emerged to enter the public domain.

However this may be in the case of religion, there would appear to be an analogous imperative arising from the dynamic of intimate relations which removes such relations from the public gaze and locates them in the domain of the private. Privacy, thus conceived, is a condition of intimacy in a sense that is at once moral-political, psychological, and ontological. Intuitively, it rings true that romantic love is fundamentally a private matter to which third parties are unwelcome. Intervention on the part of public institutions in ways that surpass the prevention of abusive treatment and the protection of rights is typically perceived as an invasion, the main exception being the institution of marriage in which the recognition of private ties assumes public form. Remaining at the level of intuition, it is not mere prudery that enjoins lovers to retreat to a private realm so that their ties may deepen and perhaps assume lasting form. It is neither modesty nor Victorian prudery that is at work here but a dynamic or structure implicit to intimacy itself.

Ultimately, the explanation for why "the state has no place in the bedrooms of the nation" stems not from the fact that the bedroom or the home is private property in which individuals may act as they wish but in the normative structure and conditions of interpersonal intimacy. If the realm of the private is conceptualized in terms of intimacy—intimate information, acts, choices, and relationships—surely sexuality would top the list of intimate acts in which the public gaze is decidedly unwelcome. If this is not intuitively evident, consider the profound distortion to intimacy that would result were such relations placed fully on public display. Such relations could hardly be described as being personal or intimate under this condition. Exclusion of outsiders and third parties seems a necessary constituent of intimate relations, as does protection from the scrutiny of public institutions.

The erotic is among the principal areas of life in which individual selves are revealed and refashioned on a basis of strong mutuality. Reaching as it does into the innermost dimensions of the personality, there is much in the area of the erotic that is variable, fragile, and requiring protection. The privacy imperative is tied directly to these qualities, yet it is not sex alone that exhibits them but the relationships that underlie it. As Charles Sykes writes,

> If we acknowledge that sex itself is a private matter, then it would seem to follow that other manifestations of those relationships of which sex is only a part also deserve protection. After all, we do not protect the privacy of sex because of the sanctified or special constitutional status of intercourse or other sex acts; we shield them because they are manifestations of the intimacies of life. It is not

> the physical act alone that is in need of protection, it is the *relationships* that lead to and shape such acts.[28]

Sykes correctly observes that in understanding fundamentally what it is in the erotic that generates the privacy imperative, it is less sexuality itself than relationships and "the intimacies of life" of which sexuality is one form of expression. This is a matter that modern culture tends to understand rather backward: it is sex, we often think, that is private, while virtually all other relationship matters are available to public inspection and, if expedient, regulation. If the utilitarian calculus or the findings of social scientific research dictate public intervention into the erotic, such is the rational course. Likewise, if the moral convictions of the majority proscribe certain forms of intimate relationships, democratic law legitimately overrides the privacy of the latter.

It is not uncommon for traditional moral-political thinking to get first things last and last things first, as this example well illustrates. What is morally primary in the realm of the erotic is not sex acts but the personal relationships from which such acts emerge, and which is the source of whatever meaning they hold. In the case of homosexuality, traditional moral thinking fixates upon the sexual act, which it presumes to be primary, and almost willfully overlooks the ground and meaning of the act. Yet, as with sexuality in the heterosexual context, it is the qualities of intimacy, affection, and strong mutuality that are morally salient. No less primary are acts of self-creation that are bound up with erotic expression. As one writer puts it,

> Being queer is more than setting up house, sleeping with a person of the same gender, and seeking state approval for doing so. It is an identity, a culture with many variations. It is a way of dealing with the world by diminishing the constraint of gender roles that have for so long kept women and gay people oppressed and invisible. Being queer means pushing the parameters of sex, sexuality, and family, and in the process transforming the very fabric of society.[29]

From the point of view of intimacy, it is irrelevant whether the parties to a relationship are of opposite genders or the same. Both instances involve the same mutuality of affection and identity in which romantic love consists. Ontologically speaking, intimacy calls into play the whole being of two selves and involves an intermingling of identities and personal boundaries more profound than in other forms of interpersonal relationship. This has long been understood at the level of metaphor. Aristophanes in Plato's *Symposium* proffers an interpretation of love as the reunion of two halves of a single hermaphroditic soul, a suggestive metaphor of the ontological affinity that love involves. In more modern times, the character of Cathy in Emily Brontë's

Wuthering Heights declares of her lover: "I *am* Heathcliff—he's always, always in my mind—not as a pleasure, any more than I am always a pleasure to myself—but as my own being." Romantic love sets in motion processes of both mutual recognition and mutual identity formation. The boundaries and terminus of the self undergo profound transformation, rendering both individuals modified as separate persons as well as participants in a shared identity. These processes presuppose openness, reciprocity, and a degree of self-knowledge but nothing specific in terms of gender or sexual orientation.

Robert Solomon, along similar lines, defends a conception of romantic love as "a dialectical process of (mutually) reconceived selfhood,"[30] as does Thomas Nagel in the context of an analysis of sexual perversion. The normal sexual relationship, which Nagel predictably opposes to the perverse, exhibits an important dimension of two-person reciprocity. Normal eroticism is conceived in antithetical terms with narcissism or the captivity of the self within its own desire. It is a dialectic of emotions and attitudes, a reaching beyond the boundaries of the self in active concern for the other's being. The normal and the perverse, accordingly, are conceived by Nagel not in terms of physical acts but at a level of psychology, perversions being "truncated or incomplete versions of the complete figuration."[31] Necrophilia, to take an obvious example, constitutes a perversion for Nagel for reason of the evident impossibility of psychological or emotional reciprocity between the living and the dead. The reciprocity of which Nagel speaks, however, is more appropriately located at the level of ontology than psychology. It is not solely, or even primarily, emotions that are at stake in the dialectic of which Nagel speaks but the whole being of the participants to a relationship. Recalling Roger Scruton's critique of homosexuality alluded to earlier—in which gay intimacy is described as narcissistic in principle on account of the absence of psychosexual distance between partners—the psychological account that he provides displays at least the virtue of moving the analysis of homosexuality to a level more profound than physical behavior, the level upon which traditional morality fixates. Its shortcoming, as with Nagel's, is to fail to move it to a level more fundamental still—the level of ontology.

The erotic puts into play not only the raw physicality and "emotional needs" of the individual but the whole being of two persons. The dialectic in which they become caught up engages their very existence in all its dimensions. The self-identity and personal boundaries of two "existing subjects" (as the existentialists would say) are called into question along with one's fundamental manner of being-in-the-world. This most elemental form of relationship is characterized by an openness in which nothing within the self is held back, no wall is unscalable, even as both preserve their identities and beings as separate persons. The psychological narcissism of which Scruton speaks undoubtedly constitutes a distortion or a failing in such a relationship, yet there is nothing in the nature of homosexuality that makes such a distortion necessary, nor is narcissism unknown among heterosexuals. More important, no matter what psychological shortcomings the parties to intimate relationships may exhibit—and who is without them?—processes of mutual recognition and identity formation transpire largely behind the back of psychology, as very often of the participants themselves. It is these very qualities of ontological affinity, mutuality, and structural symmetry that radical feminists lament as being absent from traditional male-female relationships. Some, such as Ti-Grace Atkinson, despair of even the possibility of such values, with sexuality being perceived as irredeemably ideological and oppressive to women.[32] For this writer, there is nothing in sexual love that is not explicitly political, male dominated, and humiliating. This being a matter of some necessity for Atkinson, no hope of a happier state of affairs is to be found. On a less extreme note, many other feminist authors equally lament the asymmetry of romantic love as it has been known through the ages while holding out the ideal of egalitarian reciprocity as a prospect worth striving for. A more influential feminist, Shulamith Firestone, concurs with Atkinson's critique of nonegalitarian sexuality while anticipating as a possibility at the very least the liberation of women's sexuality and the prospect of genuine equality.[33] If traditional sexuality is characterized by an unhealthy psychological dependency on the part of women and an equally pathological will to power on the part of men, perhaps a future conception of romantic love could approximate genuine mutuality and symmetry—a prospect that is hardly difficult to envision. The idea of sexual equality that has emerged from some feminist circles over the past generation is invulnerable to serious objection and is today widely proclaimed even by many of the uninitiated. Within such circles sexual equality is a political ideal, and while for my part I would concur that it is a normative ideal worth striving for, it is also more than this. It belongs within an ontological account of the very structure of intimacy itself. Structural symmetry—together with mutual recognition, openness, affinity, and identity formation—forms an ontological account of romantic love and of what happens to us (behind our backs, as it were) when we partake of it.

At this level of analysis, there is nothing that distinguishes eroticism in its homosexual and heterosexual forms, with the gender of the parties involved being of less ultimate significance than the existential processes in which they become caught up. The main difference between these forms of intimacy occurs only at the public level, where heterosexual partners are able to seek and receive recognition for their standing as a couple with some ease while gay and lesbian partners are denied such recognition. Recognition, as Hegel taught us, is not a contingent issue where self-identity is concerned, nor is it a trifling matter for romantic partnerships. The heterosexual couple presents a unified face to the world and under all but the most unusual circumstances is recognized as such. Public recognition confirms in profound ways not only the intrinsic value of the relationship but the mutual identity that the couple has fashioned. The gay or lesbian couple presents a similar face to the world and is greeted typically with a refusal of recognition and with hostility in a moral guise.

The imperative of privacy in intimate relations cuts across divisions of sexual orientation just as it cuts across divisions of race and ethnicity, culture and belief, and all other differences that separate people into opposing factions. The principles of toleration and freedom in religion have their source in the private nature of religiosity; romantic intimacy is no less a private matter, and for much the same reasons, no matter the weight of custom that limits this to majority-sanctioned practices.

CIVIL RIGHTS AND SEXUAL ORIENTATION

The movement for gay rights in essence wishes to replace the philosophy of concealment with one of equality and freedom in the domain of sexual orientation. Particular civil rights at stake in this debate include rights against discrimination in employment, housing, and military service, as well as rights to marry and to adopt children. In general terms it is a movement that seeks liberation from discrimination and harassment, particularly in their public or state-sanctioned forms. This movement began to gain momentum in the 1950s, when the British government commissioned the Wolfenden Committee to investigate and report to parliament on the subject of laws regarding prostitution and homosexuality within that nation. Delivered in 1957, the Wolfenden report advocated among its recommendations the decriminalization of homosexual acts between consenting adults and, more specifically, between gay men, with the same relations between women having already been a matter on which the law was silent. The report was soundly defeated in the British House of Commons in 1960. Of enduring significance, however, was the line of reasoning that generated its principal recommendations.

The authors of the report observed that as British law stood at the time homosexual relations between men were a criminal offense, while lesbianism, adultery, prostitution, and "fornication" were not. There being no evident basis in principle for legislating against one such moral offense and not the others, some basis would need to be found. The authors found this in an application of the public/private distinction and argued that sexual practices between consenting adults are properly outside the law regardless of how such practices stand from the point of view of common morality. Homosexuality, the report concluded, was "not the law's business"[34] provided that homosexual acts occur in private and on a consensual basis (provisions, of course, that applied equally to heterosexual practices). In the tradition of John Stuart Mill, the Wolfenden report upheld a conception of the criminal law as existing for the purpose of protecting individuals from harm rather than for the general purpose of enforcing the moral beliefs of the majority. Criminal law was limited in principle to the public domain, while the private sphere was governable by the moral choices of the individual. This philosophical statement of the relation between morality and criminal law would fare better in the decades that followed than would the report's specific policy recommendations.

Later decades saw a variety of nations adopt a similar conception of criminal law as it pertained to homosexuality and questions of sexual morality. Currently, British law holds that consensual "sodomy" between men is not a crime provided that both persons are over the age of twenty-one—although (oddly enough) the same act involving a man and a woman remains a criminal offense. In nations such as France, Sweden, the Netherlands, Denmark, and Canada, sodomy is not a crime, and gays and lesbians currently live under far fewer legal and social restrictions than in former times. In the United States the situation is decidedly less favorable. While, for instance, from the 1960s through the 1990s many states repealed statutes that had rendered sodomy a criminal offense, approximately one half elected not to do so. The reasoning behind the decision of the latter group of states is intriguing. At present antisodomy laws where they exist in the United States are largely unenforced, yet they remain on the books not out of simple inertia or legislative oversight but for a reason. That reason is to express public hostility toward lesbians and gay men, particularly the latter. The purpose of antisodomy laws is not to curtail the practice but to make a public statement of contempt for sexual orientations and practices disapproved by a majority of citizens and by Christian morality. Other laws exist for the same purpose. Approximately one half of American states, for example, make adultery a crime, while prostitution remains a crime virtually everywhere in America. Cohabitation by unmarried couples is illegal in many states, as is heterosexual sodomy between married and unmarried persons alike.[35] Again, many such laws are largely unenforced, and again public insult is their main purpose.

Of particular note in the American context is a decision of the U.S. Supreme Court in 1986 that upheld Georgia's antisodomy law, specifically refusing to apply privacy law upheld by the Court in a variety of contexts involving family, sexual morality, and related issues to homosexuality. The famous case of *Bowers v. Hardwick* challenged a Georgia law that states, "A person commits the offense of sodomy when he performs or submits to any sexual act involving the sex organs of one person and the mouth or anus of another." As worded, the statute makes no distinction between gay and heterosexual sodomy, or indeed that between unmarried and married persons; however, the Court chose to confine its attention to gay sexuality alone. The state of Georgia argued that the purpose of the law was less to ban the practice, or practices, than it was to be "symbolic." Speaking for the majority, Justice White announced, "The Constitution does not confer a fundamental right upon homosexuals to engage in sodomy. None of the fundamental rights announced in this Court's prior cases involving family relationships, marriage, or procreation bear any resemblance to the right asserted in this case." Echoing Patrick Devlin, White asserted that "the law . . . is constantly based on notions of morality, and if all laws representing essentially moral choices are to be invalidated under the Due Process Clause, the courts will be very busy indeed." While the constitution of the United States is silent on the issue of privacy (as one would expect given its eighteenth-century origins), a combination of statutes and court rulings in recent decades has created a de facto right to privacy with applications in such domains as information, education, marriage, family, reproduction, and abortion. Each of these domains is governed by the principle of free choice in matters of an intimate nature to the individual or to small groups of persons. The Supreme Court in 1986 saw no connection between heterosexual intimacies and homosexual intimacies, no common denominator in virtue of which the latter would receive the same privacy protection as that enjoyed by the former.

That a certain willful blindness was at work in the Court's reasoning is not difficult to discern. The common denominator—if it is not self-evident—is intimacy involving consenting adults in matters of sexual morality and expression. This realization was not lost on the Court's dissenting minority. Speaking for the minority, Justice Harry Blackmun found the Georgia law in contravention of principles of autonomy and privacy recognized in other areas of law involving sexual morality and intimacy. The common denominator unrecognized by the Court's majority was the principle of free choice in issues of this general nature. The minority specifically rejected religious justifications of antisodomy laws, noting that states that appeal to such justifications undermine their claim to religious neutrality.

The fact that legal prohibitions of homosexual conduct are seldom enforced—along with numerous other archaic laws, including several of those mentioned here—is often taken as evidence of the harmlessness of such laws, and without question they cause less harm in their unenforced state than when actively enforced. It bears repeating, however, that the real intent of such laws is different from law's usual purpose: it is to insult as much as, or more than, it is to prevent any identifiable harm. Legal symbolism, moreover, is far from irrelevant to judicial rulings and public policy. Very often such seemingly ethereal matters maintain a profound hold on the general spirit of public life and legal practice, effectively creating a culture of intolerance with a moral face and awarding credibility to what is in the final analysis a form of bigotry. As one observer notes, "archaic legal language also has an effect simply by staying on the books and helping to create the air of unreality in which medieval moral judgments are given authority."[36] More concretely, the fact that such laws were declared constitutional as recently as 1986 lends legal and (in the minds of many) moral credibility to legal and social disabilities imposed upon gays. In the American context these have long included exclusion from employment in the military, positions involving national security, federal judgeships, and teaching in the public school system—forms of employment all associated in the American consciousness with status and dignity. Gays and lesbians have also suffered disadvantages in the fields of adoption and child custody, again sending the unambiguous message that such persons are morally corrupting and unfit for positions of authority, particularly over children. In essence, legal and social disadvantages that are the lot of gays and lesbians in the United States and elsewhere are so many public expressions of private disdain for what are held to be a subaltern order of humanity. The overturning of antisodomy laws by the U.S. Supreme Court in 2003—on privacy grounds—is certainly a welcome development, and a drastic departure from earlier policy, yet it is perhaps too soon to know how dramatically that ruling will affect other areas of social policy in the United States.

Another area of law in which gays and lesbians have long suffered disadvantage internationally is the field of antidiscrimination law, although here again evidence of a general trend toward protection from discrimination is increasingly apparent. Recent years have seen a host of nations expressly prohibit discrimination based on sexual orientation in constitutional and statutory law. Presently the constitutions of South Africa, Germany, and Brazil include such a prohibition; the Canadian constitution as well prohibits discrimination based on "sex," which judicial interpretation has broadened to include sexual orientation. Legislative reform to the same end, particularly within the last two decades, has occurred in Australia, New Zealand, France, Sweden, Denmark, Norway, the Netherlands, Ireland, and Israel, among other nations, as well as in several American states. In international law the International Covenant on Civil and Political Rights includes both antidiscrimination and privacy provisions, the second of which formed the basis of a ruling of the United Nations Human Rights Committee in 1994 that struck down a Tasmanian law prohibiting homosexual activity between men. The European

Convention on Human Rights also proscribes discrimination based on "sex" while recognizing an individual's "right to respect for his private and family life, his home and his correspondence."[37] From this legislative perspective it would appear that state-sponsored intolerance of homosexuality is in retreat around the world, particularly in the post-1989 world of expanding human rights and globalization, which makes parochial attitudes of this kind more difficult to sustain. Yet from another—no less illuminating—perspective such legislative reform has paralleled other, less promising developments within the political culture of many nations.

In combination, such developments constitute a kind of official or public opposition to homosexuality, one that while perhaps accepting the gay fact as such, is determined to go only so far in eliminating discrimination. If anything, popular intolerance of homosexuality has been galvanized by the policy of official—and limited—tolerance, the proverbial ebb to the flow noted earlier. As one commentator remarks, "official homophobia is very prevalent but often difficult to identify. It usually takes the form of recognizing or benefitting heterosexuality and refusing similar recognition to homosexuals and homosexuality. The most common examples of this treatment involve benefits issues."[38] Same-sex partners continue to be refused benefits afforded to married persons in areas of taxation, insurance, immigration and naturalization, adoption, child custody, housing, visitation rights in hospitals and prisons, and so on. Discrimination in employment remains commonplace. (In the United States, a bill that would have rendered illegal employment discrimination against gays was defeated in 1996 at the very time that the Defense of Marriage Act—designed to prevent legal recognition of same-sex marriage—was passed.) Gays continue to face formidable obstacles in the teaching profession, most obviously in religious schools where the condemnation of homosexual "lifestyles" is routine. Very often the same religious conservatives who are long accustomed to defending religious freedom as well as religious education are equally accustomed to condemning freedom of sexual orientation, particularly in educational settings.

The principles of moral and legal equality place an onus of justification on those who would practice discrimination, whether in employment or other areas of public life. In general terms, discrimination based on sexual orientation is prima facie unjust, exceptions to this principle requiring strong justifications. Such justifications have long been proffered by the military in the United States and elsewhere, often with success. Here the argument that has found the greatest purchase concerns military effectiveness and morale in the event that open gays and lesbians be permitted to serve. The argument is succinctly stated, and defended, by Michael Levin as follows:

> Homosexuals have no place in the military if they weaken morale, and there are good reasons to think they do. First, the physical aggressiveness necessary for fighting is associated with the male personality. Women have never demonstrated the physical or psychological ability to endure sustained combat, and since homosexuals do not display the full male personality, putting them among men who do is likely to be disruptive. Second, the young, highly aggressive male who makes the paradigm soldier characteristically prides himself on his virility; he likes to brag about his athletic and, above all, sexual exploits. He will feel uncomfortable with homosexuals, and placing an open homosexual among a group of young men of this sort spells trouble. Third, combat units depend upon the sort of male bonding that also unites athletic teams. Once again, homosexual males do not display the requisite personality.[39]

The argument is premised on a host of assumptions regarding gender and sexual orientation that have become widely contested to say the least. Its central point—that some soldiers "will feel uncomfortable with homosexuals"—scarcely warrants serious consideration; by the same logic women, racial minorities, and many others who do not conform to the "paradigm soldier" ideal or whose presence might be unsettling to the chauvinistic or narrow-minded should also be excluded from military service. The same logic entails that such groups should also be discriminated against in other employment contexts in which morale and effectiveness are important to an organization (which is to say everywhere). The military effectiveness of nations that no longer practice this form of discrimination—including Germany, France, the Netherlands, Sweden, and Switzerland—appears to have withstood the threat that gays pose to morale. Of course, the kind of argument that Levin provides—and which one often hears repeated by military policymakers and politicians—is a thin rationalization of animosity and little besides.

The object of the various legal and social disabilities with which gays and lesbians have long been burdened is to insult the dignity of persons so constituted, an aim that cannot achieve success without refusing the distinction between public and private as it pertains to sexual orientation. If persons of different sexual orientations are morally and legally equal, or if the issue of sexual orientation is a private matter about which public policy is appropriately silent, then the possibility of public "statements" of opposition to homosexuality is foreclosed. It is for this reason that homosexuality, unlike many other issues of sexual morality, is not traditionally regarded as a matter of interpersonal intimacy but a public vice, closer in this respect to public indecency or pedophilia than to heterosexual intimacy.

When the proposition that homosexual acts between consenting adults are private matters about which law ought to be silent was rejected by the British parliament in 1960 and the U.S. Supreme Court in 1994, more was in play than conventional political and legal reasoning. Here is an issue that calls into play not only ancient religious sentiments but a host of psychological forces, not all of which belong among the nobler dimensions of human nature. What the issue ultimately turns upon is the distinction between public affairs and private life and specifically the possibility of respect for private differences that are fundamental to our being. Sexual orientation is not alone in this regard; gender, religious, ethnic, and cultural differences of several kinds are equally fundamental to the self-understandings that orient human existence, yet this issue stands virtually alone among such differences insofar as liberal democracies continue to insist that sexual orientation belongs within the domain of public affairs—and for reasons that apply neither more nor less to this than to the other private differences noted. Public assaults on the dignity of religious or ethnic minorities have become unthinkable in contemporary political culture. For politicians, open expression of disrespect for such differences is the surest route to electoral defeat, indicating the distance that many nations have traveled from the times of racial or religious warfare. What made it possible for modern constitutional democracies to resolve such disputes were principles of equal freedom and respect for private differences, irrespective of popular disapproval or bigotry with respect to such differences. It is the same principles that underlie the movement for gay rights.

SAME-SEX MARRIAGE

Remaining on the topic of discrimination, the one form of this that continues to receive widespread legislative and popular support is in the field of marriage law, evidenced by the fact that only four nations in the world (Belgium, the Netherlands, and—as of 2005—Canada and Spain[40]) recognize in full the right of gay and lesbian marriage and by the legislative lengths to which certain nations have recently gone to prevent such recognition. The debate over same-sex marriage warrants close attention not only as an illustration of antidiscrimination law in many nations but for the reason that it is an issue uniquely rich in symbolism and indicative of what is ultimately at stake in all political discourse regarding sexual orientation. As one American party to this debate has observed, "granting homosexuals entrance into this institution is tantamount to complete acceptance of homosexuality by American [or any] society. No other measure would signal approval in such a stark and unambiguous way."[41] If antigay sentiments have become somewhat antique politically, the institution of marriage constitutes the antiquarian's final refuge. At stake in this rather rancorous debate is far more than the practical benefits that the marriage institution has long afforded heterosexual couples; indeed, what is ultimately at stake is essentially no different from what I have been arguing is invariably at stake in gay rights issues: public acceptance of difference or its refusal. What distinguishes same-sex marriage from the other issues noted here is less a matter of principle than one of degree of explicitness—whether majorities are prepared to tolerate and perhaps respect what tradition had deemed as sin.

A brief look at legislation governing same-sex relationships in different nations reveals evidence of slow movement toward some form of public or legal recognition, although no less interesting are the forms that such recognition takes. Several European states (including France, Germany, Denmark, Sweden, and Norway) currently recognize in law registered partnerships, benefits of which include some but not all of those associated with marriage. While varying between nations, such benefits often include rights regarding taxation and inheritance, adoption, insurance, pensions, unemployment benefits, and partner support in the event of separation. Typically, registered partnerships are accorded benefits and status that more closely approximate those of heterosexual common-law relationships than marriage, evidenced by the selective nature of the prerogatives and responsibilities that are accorded such partnerships.

Court rulings in the United States have largely refused petitions of gay couples for the right to marry. Recent years have seen vigorous debate over this issue, particularly in the wake of a ruling in 1993 by the Supreme Court of Hawaii which held that prohibiting same-sex marriage violates the principle of equal rights, as well as a similar ruling in Massachusetts in 2004. Both rulings caused no little stir among federal legislators, the former leading directly to the Defense of Marriage Act of 1996 and the latter leading to President Bush's proposal for a constitutional amendment explicitly banning same-sex marriage. The Defense of Marriage Act defined marriage in explicit terms as an arrangement between two persons of opposite genders, as well as providing that states may refuse recognition of same-sex marriages of other states. As if this did not suffice, a 1998 referendum in Hawaii permitted the state legislature to amend its constitution in order to explicitly prohibit gay and lesbian marriage. Similar referenda conducted during the 2004 elections provided popular support for amendments to state constitutions in all eleven states in which the idea was proposed.

At the risk of stating the obvious, the motivation of such legislative activity is not what it purports to be. The standard argument appealed to by the traditional restrictive conception of marriage is a kind of definitional argument that by fiat limits the meaning of the term to heterosexual partnerships. Hence the Defense of Marriage Act states, "the word 'marriage' means only a legal union between one man and one woman as husband and wife, and the word 'spouse' refers only to a person of the opposite sex who is a husband or a wife." The definitional stipulation is normally supplemented with a second stipulation, concerning the meaning and purpose of marriage. This singular purpose is procreation. As Jean Bethke Elshtain states,

> Marriage is not, and never has been, primarily about two people—it is and always has been about the possibility of generativity. Although in any given instance, a marriage might not have led to the raising of a family, whether through choice or often unhappy recognition of, and final reconciliation to, the infertility of one or another spouse, the symbolism of marriage-family as social regenesis is fused in our centuries-old experience with marriage ritual, regulation, and persistence.[42]

Similar sentiments are routinely expressed by politicians, clergy, and activists, not all of whom are conservative. Speaking in a debate in the U.S. Senate in 1996, for example, West Virginia senator Robert Byrd argued,

> To insist that male-male or female-female relationships must have the same status as the marriage relationship is more than unwise, it is patently absurd. Out of such relationships children do not result. Of course, children do not always result from marriages as we have traditionally known them. But out of same-sex relationships no children can result.[43]

It is not only on the floor of legislatures that definitional fiat and emotionally charged language are frequent substitutes for argumentation, yet insofar as what we have here is an argument, it is one that is vulnerable to criticism on several grounds.

On a historical note, it is far from evident that procreation defines the purpose of the institution of marriage. Historically, marriage is no less an affair of property and social status than it is one of children. Before the romantic era, its main purpose was as much a business transaction as it was the genesis of a family; however, since that era its defining purpose and meaning are primarily conceived as the romantic love of two persons, whether the couple eventually produces children or not. In addition, defining the raison d'être of marriage as procreation spells trouble for the countless married couples who remain childless either by intention or necessity. That such couples nonetheless participate in the symbolism of "social regenesis," as Elshtain asserts, is logically gymnastic, particularly in view of the number of gay and lesbian parents and adoptive situations that exhibit no more evidence of parental incompetence than their heterosexual counterparts. Third, definitional stipulation merely begs the question that is at issue. If the question of same-sex marriage is to be resolved, it will be resolved on ethical-political, not semantic or quasi-historical, grounds.

The traditional restrictive view of marriage is principally motivated not by a child-centered conception of the meaning and purpose of the institution but by a familiar form of will to power which is the will of majorities to exclude and deride minorities. This unusually transparent form of will to power operates according to the following logic: homosexual intimacy is profoundly threatening to many—traditionally a majority of—persons for reasons more psychological than ethical; it must therefore be relegated to the margins of social life, a move that must be justified in ethical-political terms; since religious morality is no longer sufficient to this public purpose, a basis in secular morality must be found. It is here that the child-centered theory of marriage makes its appearance and is asserted to be a matter of either historical or a priori truth.

If there is a truth of any kind to be glimpsed through the subterfuge that surrounds this issue, it is that heterosexual majorities are not willing to accept that homosexual relationships merit equal respect to heterosexual ones, that while popular conceptions of gay and lesbian partnerships are gradually liberalizing in many parts of the world, the recognition of full equality remains somewhat off in the distance. Popular attitudes on this subject are slow to change, yet from the point of view of the state the presumption against discrimination and publicly supported class structures is fundamental to a social order that prizes equal rights. As Frederick Elliston remarks, law's "failure to include homosexual marriages can be regarded as a failure to provide freedom in one of its most important areas—our intimate, personal sexual life. The fact that some cannot marry the partner of their choice marks a moral deficiency in our society."[44] While gay and lesbian activists remain divided on the question of the desirability of marriage, given its appearance to many as an inherently oppressive and sexist institution, the right to participate in it for those who view it in a more favorable light is enjoined by principles of nondiscrimination and equal freedom in matters profoundly private in nature.

WHICH FAMILY? WHOSE VALUES?

A debate closely related to the one I have been discussing concerns the general area of family and its contemporary transformations or, as traditionalists prefer, "breakdown." The movement for gay rights—together with increasing rates of divorce, single parenthood, abortion, and so on—is frequently cited as evidence of the decline of what American conservatives call "family values," a popular euphemism for traditional Christian morality. Religious conservatives urge a return of sorts to an era or mind-set in which families included two married and opposite-gendered parents, religious faith was more prevalent, divorce was uncommon, and homosexuals assumed a less visible presence in the social landscape. Central to this form of conservatism is a defense of "family," where the term signifies exclusively the traditional Christian conception of family and the values associated with it. As one American senator expresses it,

> In every major religion in history, from the early Greek myths of the *Iliad* and the *Odyssey* to the oldest writings of the Bible to the oldest teachings of civilization, governments have recognized the traditional family as the foundation of prosperity and happiness, and in democratic societies, as the foundation of freedom. Human beings have always given traditional marriage a special sanction. Not that there cannot be contracts among individuals, but there is something unique about the traditional family in terms of what it does for our society and the foundation it provides—this is something that every civilized society in five thousand years of recorded history has recognized.[45]

Variations of the traditional family, in this often-encountered view, are either prefixed families or nonfamilies. In particular, "homosexual 'families,'" in Michael Levin's words, "are in the strictest sense unnatural,"[46] a sentiment regularly upheld (if not always publicly stated) by religious conservatives.

The traditional family movement is the most recent incarnation of the evangelicalism previously noted that has long characterized American political culture. In communitarian fashion it singles out for public recognition a particular conception of the good life—the life of home and hearth, of faith in God and country—and fashions an array of incentives and disincentives for persons to marry and procreate. The broad aim of public policy in this area is to reward married heterosexuals who embody this ideal and to discipline the rest. Gays and lesbians, single parents, adulterers, and unwed couples already accustomed to moral censure become objects of social engineering. This communitarian measure, as one critic states, "brings the machinery of administration to bear on the realm of pleasures and intimate relations, aiming to stifle variety among ways of living. It authorizes the state to make one form of life—*already normative*—even more privileged."[47]

When it is an aim of government to produce conformity in private lives to a particular conception of virtue, the price it exacts with respect to privacy, equality, and freedom itself is high. When its aim is the nostalgic one of returning to the settled habits or ways of thinking of a prior era, it is deceiving itself about what is historically possible. One of the realities of modern life is that homogeneity in virtually all its forms has been replaced by plurality. Sameness of belief, values, culture, race, sexual orientation, and so on, has become a relic of a bygone age, and while many conservatives may lament this fact or look back to a time in which homogeneity was the rule rather than the exception, it is not for government to follow suit. The contemporary reality is that family has assumed a variety of forms, no one of which captures the essence of its meaning. While several of these are yet to receive public recognition, nontraditional conceptions of family are not temporary aberrations but part of the general movement of social life toward increasing complexity and multiplicity.

The same movement carries implications for marriage. Once a monolithic institution with both legal and religious dimensions, marriage has become as much a secular affair as a theological one. The religious component once deemed by tradition to be an ineluctable component of marriage is now a decidedly optional matter, as is the permanence of marital union, the raising of children, and so on. Perhaps it is this that many of the conservative-minded find so profoundly disturbing: that what was once thought immutable and uniform has become a contingency or, even more unsettling, that a contingency it has always been. When religionists and others speak of "family" and "values" as if these terms admit of neither ambiguity nor plurality, a political psychology of nostalgia and, more frequently than not, intolerance is plainly visible.

In discussions of public policy the move toward psychological "explanations" of political opinions not one's own is appropriately undertaken in only exceptional cases. The social critic who habitually "diagnoses" rather than critiques judgments and practices to which he or she is opposed is often vulnerable to the charge of bad faith or false authority, yet in the present context questions of psychological explanation seem apposite. The psychological note on which opposition to gay rights is most often expressed is decidedly more shrill than what is usual in political discourse. Consider as a case in point one contemporary philosopher's words on the subject of homosexuals and discrimination:

> It is perfectly rational for an employer to want to avoid [repellent] personalities and rational for him to believe that hiring homosexuals creates a greater risk of being saddled with one. Or consider a landlord disinclined to rent to homosexuals because of his reasonable and correct belief that homosexuals are much more promiscuous than heterosexuals. He may fear, again reasonably, that promiscuous tenants attract strangers who will threaten security and be heedless of his property. He may worry that homosexuals, ever on the prowl, will keep late hours annoying to other tenants, who themselves prefer heterosexual neighbors. The landlord may consider homosexuals unclean, another reasonable concern given the data about venereal disease. Homosexuality is a valid, information-rich proxy. Laws against "arbitrary" discrimination, even if they survived Mill's [harm] principle, would permit discrimination based on sexual preference.[48]

The same author writes that traditionalists, of whom he is one,

> *deplore* homosexuality, and like most people they utilize the language of disapprobation that is handiest, namely moral disapprobation, to express themselves. But what they really mean is that homosexuality is disgusting, nauseating, closely connected with fecal matter. One need not show that anal intercourse is immoral to be warranted in wanting to be as far away from it as possible.[49]

To say that the tone of this author's remarks, and of many similar from him, is not one of scholarly argumentation is to understate the matter dramatically. It is closer to what one used to expect from the more strident among religious conservatives, although politicians who harbor such attitudes today would be foolish so to express them on the public record. Consider as well the words of noted philosopher and theologian Karl Barth: "[Homosexuality] is the physical, psychological and social sickness, the phenomenon of perversion, decadence and decay, which can emerge when man refuses to admit the validity of the divine command in the sense in which we are now considering it."[50] That professional philosophers would resort to such vitriol reveals much about the psychological forces that this issue calls into play for so many.

The intolerance that many feel toward gays and lesbians, which is barely contained beneath the surface of many efforts to "defend" marriage and the traditional family, prefers to articulate itself in the language of morality, yet no specially acute powers of perception are required to see that it is plain revulsion and animosity that underlie this form of traditionalism. Opposition to civil rights for homosexuals is typically unlike political opposition in its usual forms—to tax increases, for example, or health care reform. Its origins lie in deeper psychological waters than do the more standard forms of political opposition or social criticism, and it is this that calls for explanation. Critics of gay rights who appeal to scriptural authority are unable to explain why the venom they direct toward homosexuality—particularly toward gay men—far outstrips their condemnation of divorce or bearing false witness, acts proscribed with equal or greater severity in biblical texts. Defenders of family life are similarly unable to explain why their animosity toward gays dramatically exceeds their animosity toward abusive spouses or incompetent parents. Surely spousal and child abuse pose no less a threat to family life than does homosexuality, yet opposition to the former among social conservatives is rather muted in comparison with their intolerance of gays and lesbians.

It is the nature of contempt, as of hatred, that its object is never without a certain relation to its subject. "It is a logical feature of contempt," as Laurence Thomas observes, "that we cannot have contempt for that which it is psychologically impossible for us to be and which has no bearing at all on what we might be."[51] Thomas is surely correct in his observation, as a century of psychological investigation bears out. An object of contempt represents, symbolically at the very least, something that is within us to become and which, were we to become it, would contravene our present mode of self-understanding. The threat that homosexuality represents is neither to the moral fiber of the society nor to the institutions of marriage and family but to the psychological integrity of certain heterosexual personalities. Sexual difference confronts us with the realization, unsettling to many, that our sexuality is not fixed in the firmament but is a contingency—that our sexual identity and orientation might have been otherwise, that intimacy assumes a range of forms far broader than that recognized by traditional moralists. While many such moralists have since ancient times anxiously willed it otherwise and urged the confinement of sexuality to marriage (and even there to specific acts), and while to this day the urgency of thinking ourselves "normal" in this facet of our existence above all others is keenly felt, historians of human sexuality consistently remind us that virtually everything connected with this is quite far from absolute. Sexuality belongs no less within the rise and fall of history than do all other social phenomena. For many this is a profoundly unsettling realization even as the historical and contemporary evidence for it is compelling. The familiar fact, for example, that incarcerated persons often engage in homosexual activity while exhibiting all signs of heterosexual orientation both prior to and again after their period of incarceration suggests in the plainest terms that sexuality is neither independent of conditions—practical and historical—nor a fixed verity of our nature.

It is this fact that ultimately explains the revulsion felt by many toward homosexuality. Gays, lesbians, bisexuals, and others whose practices and orientations obscure traditional boundaries of gender compel many of those not so inclined to recognize the contingency of what they imagined unassailable within their own being. Particular relationships and their forms, sexual identities and orientations, boundaries of male and female—each of these is more fluid than conventional wisdom imagines. Our self-conceptions, still more our security, may depend on denying this fact, just as imagining in the language of psychoanalysis that the conscious ego sits firmly atop the unconscious provides illusory comfort to many, but even necessary illusions remain illusions.

Privacy and freedom in matters of interpersonal intimacy are imperatives that rightfully override majoritarian distaste or disapproval of minority practices. Where there is mutuality of consent, expressions of sexuality between adults are private matters about which majorities may express approval or disapproval as they wish, so long as it does not assume legislative form.

NOTES

1. Pierre Elliott Trudeau, *The Essential Trudeau*, ed. Ron Graham (Toronto: McClelland and Stewart, 1998), 9.

2. Trudeau, *Essential Trudeau*, 9.

3. Patrick Devlin, *The Enforcement of Morals* (Oxford: Oxford University Press, 1965), 14.

4. Devlin, *Enforcement of Morals*, 10.

5. See, for example, Devlin, *Enforcement of Morals*, 9, 17, 99. Regarding homosexuality, Devlin remarks, "There is, for example, a general abhorrence of homosexuality. We should ask ourselves in the first instance whether, looking at it calmly and dispassionately, we regard it as a vice so abominable that its mere presence is an offence. If that is the genuine feeling of the society in which we live, I do not see how society can be denied the right to eradicate it" (17).

6. Devlin, *Enforcement of Morals*, 17.

7. See Michael Levin, "Against Homosexual Liberation," in *Sexual Orientation and Human Rights*, by Michael Levin and Laurence Thomas (Lanham, Md.: Rowman & Littlefield, 1999).

8. Richard Posner, *Sex and Reason* (Cambridge, Mass.: Harvard University Press, 1992), 232.

9. Posner, *Sex and Reason*, 230.

10. See, for example, Michael Sandel, *Democracy's Discontent: America in Search of a Public Philosophy* (Cambridge, Mass.: Harvard University Press, 1996), and *Liberalism and the Limits of Justice* (Cambridge: Cambridge University Press, 1982).

11. Laurence Thomas observes, "Throughout the entire Bible the issue of homosexuality is addressed on only a handful of occasions. In his parables, Jesus never once addresses the issue. In the Old Testament account of the ongoing relationship between Israel and God, the issue of homosexuality is not at the forefront of God's concern and despair with Israel. Homosexuality is neither the major nor minor theme of any of the great prophets. When God called the children of Israel a 'stiff-necked people' (*Exodus* 32:9), it is absolutely clear that homosexual behavior on their part is not what occasioned this scathing appellation. Nor, again, is homosexuality the concern of the book of Revelation of the New Testament, the theme of which is the end of time. In particular, the letters written to the seven churches never once address the issue of homosexuality." Thomas, "The Good Society and Sexual Orientation," in Levin and Thomas, *Sexual Orientation and Human Rights*, 37.

12. Thomas, "Good Society," 37–38.

13. One philosopher who does entertain such arguments as they pertain to our subject is Thomas, who does a competent job of refuting them in "Good Society."

14. Levin, "Against Homosexual Liberation," 110.

15. Levin, "Against Homosexual Liberation," 110.

16. See Elizabeth Anscombe, "Contraception and Chastity," *Human World*, no. 7 (1972): 9–30. Also see Sara Ruddick, "On Sexual Morality," in *Moral Problems*, ed. James Rachels (New York: Harper and Row, 1975).

17. Levin, "Against Homosexual Liberation," 85.

18. As Plato writes in the *Laws*, "Our citizens should not be inferior to birds and many other species of animals, which are born in large communities and up to the age of procreation live unmated, pure and unpolluted by marriage, but when they have arrived at that age they pair, male with female and female with male, according to their inclination, and for the rest of their time they live in a pious and law-abiding way, faithfully adhering to the agreements which were the beginning of their love." Plato, *Laws* 804d–e, trans. A. E. Taylor, *The Collected Dialogues of Plato*, eds. Edith Hamilton and Huntington Cairns (Princeton, N.J.: Princeton University Press, 1961).

19. Marquis de Sade, *Justine* (New York: Grove Press, 1965), 318.

20. Mill urged this point in connection with the view common among his Victorian contemporaries that inequality between the sexes was also part of the natural order. Following the sentence cited, Mill writes, "The subjection of women to men being a universal custom, any departure from it quite naturally appears unnatural. But how entirely, even in this case, the feeling is dependent on custom, appears by ample experience." Mill, *The Subjection of Women*, in *On Liberty and Other Writings*, ed. Stefan Collini (Cambridge: Cambridge University Press, 2003), 130.

21. Levin, "Against Homosexual Liberation," 119.

22. Roger Scruton, *Sexual Desire: A Moral Philosophy of the Erotic* (New York: Free Press, 1986), 310.

23. Levin, "Against Homosexual Liberation," 129.

24. Michel Foucault, *The History of Sexuality*, vol. 1, *An Introduction*, trans. Robert Hurley (New York: Vintage Books, 1990), 43.

25. Jeremy Bentham, "An Essay on 'Paederasty,'" in *Philosophy and Sex*, eds. Robert Baker and Frederick Elliston (Buffalo, N.Y.: Prometheus Books, 1984), 354.

26. Bentham, "Essay on 'Paederasty,'" 355.

27. See H. L. A. Hart, *Law, Liberty, and Morality* (Stanford, Calif.: Stanford University Press, 1963).

28. Charles Sykes, *The End of Privacy* (New York: St. Martin's Press, 1999), 216.

29. Paula Ettelbrick, "Since When Is Marriage a Path to Liberation?" in *Same-Sex Marriage: Pro and Con*, ed. Andrew Sullivan (New York: Vintage Books, 1997), 120.

30. Robert M. Stewart, *Philosophical Perspectives on Sex and Love* (New York: Oxford University Press, 1995), 253.

31. Thomas Nagel, "Sexual Perversion," in Baker and Elliston, *Philosophy and Sex*, 276.

32. See Ti-Grace Atkinson, "Radical Feminism" and "The Institution of Sexual Intercourse," in *Notes from the Second Year: Women's Liberation* (New York: Radical Feminism, 1970).

33. See Shulamith Firestone, *The Dialectic of Sex* (New York: Bantam Books, 1970).

34. *Report of the Committee on Homosexual Offences and Prostitution*, also known as the Wolfenden report (London: HMSO, 1957), 61.

35. Legal definitions of *sodomy* range from the specific—anal intercourse between men—to the general—essentially any sexual act other than kissing and copulation.

36. Michael Warner, *The Trouble with Normal: Sex, Politics, and the Ethics of Queer Life* (New York: Free Press, 1999), 13.

37. See article 8 of the European Convention on Human Rights.

38. Bruce MacDougall, *Queer Judgments: Homosexuality, Expression, and the Courts in Canada* (Toronto: University of Toronto Press, 2000), 180.

39. Levin, "Against Homosexual Liberation," 128.

40. At the time of this writing, the Canadian government has passed legislation legalizing same-sex marriage. The move was prompted by a ruling of the Canadian Supreme Court in 2004 that declared the ban on such marriages unconstitutional as well as similar rulings in seven of Canada's ten provincial supreme courts in 2003 and 2004. As Canadian justice minister Irwin Cotler has remarked, "Canada is a land built on a tradition of equality and respect. It is the responsibility of Parliament to ensure that minority rights are uniform across the country. The government cannot and should not pick and choose which rights they will defend and which rights they will ignore" ("Canada Considers National Same-Sex Marriage," www.billingsgazette.com, February 2, 2005). Speaking on the evening of the vote in the House of Commons, prime minister Paul Martin noted, "We are a nation of minorities. And in a nation of minorities, it is important that you don't cherry-pick rights. A right is a right and that is what this vote tonight is all about" ("Same-Sex Marriage Bill Passes Commons Vote," www.ctv.ca, July 20, 2005). The bill states that "marriage, for civil purposes, is the lawful union of two persons to the exclusion of all others." Additionally, "it is recognized that officials of religious groups are free to refuse to perform marriages that are not in accordance with their religious beliefs." Canada's Catholic bishops and other religious leaders have loudly protested the new law. As one Catholic archbishop has recently stated, "this is not a human rights issue; it is about recognizing the biological basis for the social structure that protects the procreation and nurturing of children in our society." The tolerance that such a law calls for, states the archbishop, "is a false tolerance." A different archbishop has warned in a letter to prime minister Paul Martin that legalizing same-sex marriage "will be teaching that homosexual activity and heterosexual activity are morally equivalent" ("Canada Braces for a Social Tsunami," www.zenit.org, February 5, 2005). Still another Catholic archbishop declares that the law "threatens to unleash nothing less than cultural upheaval whose negative consequences are still impossible to predict" ("Canadian Same-Sex Marriage No Sure Thing," www.gaycitynews.com, February 9, 2005). Pope John Paul II also waded into the debate, remarking that same-sex marriage belongs to "a new ideology of evil": "It is legitimate and necessary to ask oneself," he writes, "if this is not perhaps part of a new ideology of evil, perhaps more insidious and hidden, which attempts to pit human rights against the family and against man" ("Pope Says Gay Marriage Part of 'Ideology of Evil,'" www.ctv.ca, February 23, 2005). More recently, Pope Benedict XVI has asserted, "Today's various forms of dissolution of marriage, free unions, trial marriages, as well as the pseudo-matrimonies between people of the same sex are instead expressions of anarchic freedom which falsely tries to pass itself off as the true liberation of man" ("Pope Condemns Same-Sex Marriage," www.cbc.ca, June 6, 2005). What is perhaps more remarkable than the content of these and countless similar remarks is the shrill tone with which they are so often expressed. The animosity is as palpable as it is psychologically intriguing.

41. Andrew Sullivan, "Introduction," in Sullivan, *Same-Sex Marriage*, xxii.

42. Jean Bethke Elshtain, "Against Gay Marriage," *Commonweal*, October 22, 1991.

43. Robert Byrd, Senate debate on the Defense of Marriage Act, in Sullivan, *Same-Sex Marriage*, 232.

44. Frederick Elliston, "Gay Marriage," in Baker and Elliston, *Philosophy and Sex*, 161.

45. Phil Gramm, Senate debate on the Defense of Marriage Act, in Sullivan, *Same-Sex Marriage*, 231. By "every major religion in history," of course, the senator means every major Western religion. His lack of acquaintance with several other major religious traditions is evident from this statement. One thinks of the Buddhist tradition, for instance, in which precisely the renunciation of family is fundamental to the attainment of enlightenment.

46. Levin, "Against Homosexual Liberation," 116.

47. Warner, *Trouble with Normal*, 112.

48. Levin, "Against Homosexual Liberation," 127–28.

49. Levin, "Against Homosexual Liberation," 145.

50. Karl Barth, "Church Dogmatics," in *Homosexuality and Ethics*, ed. E. Batchelor (New York: Pilgrim, 1980), 49.

51. Thomas, "Good Society," 64.

Chapter Four

Property and the Private Sphere

As previously noted, theorists have long regarded the notions of privacy and the private sphere, together with the distinction between public and private, as being ambiguous with respect to both their abstract definitions and their practical applications. One dimension of the ambiguity arises from an ancient association of the private sphere with the domain of property, whether it connotes the household or the sphere of private property more generally. Whereas the Greeks were inclined to adopt a narrow conception of the private as essentially the realm of the household, modern parlance typically broadens its definition to include other economic holdings—most notably land, yet also including a range of properties, from personal effects to capital, commercial enterprises, and so on. The claim of "private property" carries considerable normative force and puts a brake on expressions of public will that involve the disposition of private holdings. Yet what precisely is the relation between property and the private sphere? If it is not one of simple identity, as seems evident to common sense and as the arguments of preceding chapters help to elucidate, what dissimilarities and overlappings characterize their relation? How, given the proximity in both ancient and modern discourse of the domains of property and privacy, ought we conceive their relation, including both the theoretical and the principled point of distinction between these two domains as well as their overlappings in practical affairs?

Since ancient times, states frequently have operated on the premise that a domain of the private exists; that it constitutes a normative limit upon the public will; that it encompasses the marital relation, family life, and the general affairs of the household; and in modern times that it is intimately associated with economic holdings beyond house and home. The private sphere is a protected domain of the individual or of small associations of persons—including, in particular, families. By traditional decree, the household is presided over by a dominant male, whose right to protection from the scrutiny and intervention of outsiders is nearly absolute yet whose rule over other persons in the home is apolitical in nature. Indeed, philosophers have often gone to extremes in denying the political nature of the authority enjoyed by the patriarch in a traditional household—Aristotle and John Locke being notable cases in point, as we shall see in the course of our analysis. What prompts what are sometimes tortured exercises in political reasoning is the intuition—pronounced within, but not unique to, modern liberalism—that there exists a domain of autonomy rightfully belonging to the individual (or to some individuals) which includes, but is not limited to, the domestic scene. The private sphere, so conceived, possesses a physical or quasi-physical status: it is a plot of earth, a dwelling, a bedroom—something around which one could erect a fence or four walls.

While, as I argue in chapter 1, the concepts of privacy and the private sphere incorporate connotations of spatiality or social distance, the argument of this chapter cautions against interpreting such spatiality in crudely physical or otherwise simple terms. The "domain" or "sphere" of private life is a fundamentally normative, not physical or metaphysical, category. It signifies an ethical boundary and inviolability related in complex fashion to the material and the bodily. While its applications in practice bring it into frequent proximity with the realms of property and domesticity, the private sphere connotes a properly ethical space between persons, not all of whom (as should go without saying but perhaps does not) are patriarchal heads of households. Understanding privacy, I wish to argue, means understanding it in relation to property, not because the two notions are conceptually nondistinct, but because comprehending their distinction and interrelations affords some clarification to the notion of privacy itself. The task of articulating this distinction includes identifying the ethical basis of both privacy rights and property rights. Identifying similarities and dissimilarities in their respective normative justifications sheds important light on these concepts themselves, as does noting the partial yet hardly complete overlappings of their practical applications.

Accordingly, the scope of this chapter includes an analysis, first, of the ancient association of privacy with the household and domestic life; second, of property rights in their broader, modern connotation—particularly as they are articulated within liberal thought, the tradition in which such rights have long held center stage; and, finally, of a variety of property rights that are especially relevant both to our own times and to the central argument of these studies: intellectual property rights. The last provides an important application and test case of the defense of property rights that I offer in this chapter.

If the privacy imperative is in one fashion or another universal with respect to time and place, no less universal is the acquisitive impulse associated with property as well as—albeit less obviously so—a countervailing impulse which we may designate as the utopian impulse. Few if any cultures, it is true, elevate acquisition in the sense of modern economic materialism to the status of a first principle, yet the impulse to acquire and hold material objects in one's secure possession is hardly unique to modern capitalist societies. Dividing what is yours from what is mine—whether you and I are individuals in one of the several modern connotations of the term or collectivities of one or another description—is an imperative readily observable across human cultures, even while assuming a great many forms in actual practice. Yet coexisting in the human imagination with this is an impulse of an antithetical sort, a longing for arrangements in which divisions of mine and yours disappear entirely. The universal myth of a golden age of the past is of a form of social life in which, among other things, goods of every kind most often are held in common. Invariably tinged with nostalgia, this collective yearning to return to an age—real or imagined—prior to the introduction of property is traditionally couched in ethical-political terms, even as its more ultimate source likely lies in psychological waters deeper than those of moral intuition. In its several manifestations the utopian impulse speaks of an earthly paradise wherein divisions of yours and mine are unknown. Even as environmental objects are used or consumed by individuals, they belong by right to no person or perhaps to a mythical paternal figure or the collective grouping.

This abiding impulse has long afforded prima facie support for left politics. Widespread sentiment has long had it that but for unfortunate necessities and the baser elements of human nature, social reality would ideally conform to a kind of natural communism that is without socioeconomic stratification and inequalities of all kinds, where poverty and envy are unknown, and where private property is curtailed or nonexistent. The moral foundations of utopian and socialist politics accentuate premises concerning property and the inequalities and power relations to which it gives rise. The institution of property is commonly identified as the root of injustices from economic exploitation to poverty, ignorance, alienation, and a host of social ills to which abolition or redistribution of property provides the remedies. For Karl Marx and the tradition he inspired, private property constitutes the negation of human agency and the source of alienation widely visible in the Europe of his time. Indeed, as Marx and Engels express it in *The Communist Manifesto*, "the theory of the communists may be summed up in a single sentence: Abolition of private property."[1] Much the same sentiment is expressed in the socialist literature of the nineteenth and twentieth centuries. Pierre-Joseph Proudhon, for instance, famously declared that "property is theft," while other socialists of his time restated arguments proffered by Jean-Jacques Rousseau and his eighteenth-century contemporaries. Rousseau, of course (that is, at any rate, the Rousseau of *A Discourse on the Origin of Inequality* and not the Rousseau of *A Discourse on Political Economy*, in which he speaks of property as "the most sacred of all the rights of citizenship, and even more important in some respects than liberty itself"[2]), regarded private property and its unequal distribution as the chief causes of civil strife and of most every social ill that he observed. Inequalities of wealth led directly to the baser forms of envy, along with war, slavery, and other evils absent from an essentially peaceful state of nature. If it is to exist at all, private property must remain subordinate to the common good, a tenet shared by an array of socialists, communists, and others indebted to Rousseau, including many liberal theorists of the nineteenth and twentieth centuries.

Antiproprietary sentiments, of course, have ancient roots in Platonic thought as well. The guardian class and rulers of Plato's republic were to hold all things in common, not excluding wives and children, since private possession was incompatible with the virtues and a principal cause of social strife. In *The Republic* property and particularist ties were to be abolished to the extent possible and curtailed to the extent otherwise; commoners, for instance, were permitted to hold property since by nature they were appetitive and incapable of living the fully virtuous life. Here as well the utopian impulse is fully manifest, even as Plato would later temper this in *The Laws*. For Plato particularity in all its forms is morally and metaphysically debased, while abstract universality—represented politically in the form of justice and the good—is indicative of a higher order of virtue and of being, a premise that Rousseau and later thinkers of the left would appropriate in modern guise.

After its apotheosis in the capitalist economies of the nineteenth century, the right of private property came under radical assault in the communist regimes of the twentieth century, while in market societies it came under restriction in a multitude of forms. Under the influence of socialist and indeed much liberal thought, property rights lost their erstwhile status as indispensable conditions of political liberty and economic prosperity and became subject to increasing restriction in the name of the public welfare. With property and wealth being "social" commodities, socialists and liberals alike argued, the public is within its rights in reclaiming by legislative means what are essentially common products entrusted, as it were, to individual or corporate proprietors to serve the public interest. New Deal measures of the 1930s and their legislative counterparts in other market societies placed principles of property rights and contractual freedom on an increasingly contingent basis in a general spirit of utilitarian optimization or engineering aimed at the economic security of all but particularly of those victimized by economic depression. As the twentieth century unfolded, property rights became increasingly subject to the calculus of social utility and the requirements of welfare politics. Income redistribution, zoning restrictions, advertising regulations, and other legislative measures supplemented traditional qualifications of property rights, such as taxation and eminent domain—the right of government to expropriate land and other property, provided that expropriation be undertaken for an identifiable public purpose and that owners receive compensation in some form. The movement for environmental protection as well, having aligned itself from its inception with leftist politics, has tended to regard property rights as little more than ideological conditions and rationalizations of environmental degradation. If the source of such deterioration lies in private property, a familiar argument goes, the solution must lie in publicizing property or subjecting it ever more to the management of public institutions and the will of the public at large. It is a movement that has tended to dovetail, as if by logical necessity, with socialist or welfare politics, subordinating property to increasingly rigorous tests of social utility if not removing it altogether from the realms of the private and indeed of rights.[3]

Yet for all the restrictions or outright assaults that property rights have undergone over the past century, the acquisitive impulse and imperative of secure possession appear not to have abated in any appreciable degree. Even as, from the standpoint of public policy, the concept of ownership as a form of guaranteed legal right has for a century been hedged with a thousand qualifications, the concept itself, from the private or personal side of the equation, has suffered not at all. One is prompted to ask, from a "sociological" standpoint (or perhaps from one of social ontology), what accounts for what appears to be a remarkably intransigent phenomenon of our social being—that no matter the death by qualifications that they appear to have suffered, the concepts of property, ownership, and acquisition persist in the moral consciousness of global civilization? Were they mere relics of a former age, ideological obfuscations of "capital," or mechanisms of hegemony, one would expect them to dissolve into nothingness after decades of regulation and centuries of critique had exercised their effect, yet such is so far from being the case that, if anything, the reverse would seem closer to the truth. The global economy and civilization that are emerging appear not less, but more, wedded to property than at any previous time in world history. Western notions of privatization and ownership, along with individuality and human rights, are rapidly gaining recognition internationally not as parochial values of American or European culture manipulatively exported abroad but as global values appropriate to the civilization that is now emerging. What, we may inquire, is the root of the impulse to own and acquire that has forever coexisted in the human imagination with its logical contrary: the utopian impulse to dissolve divisions of mine and yours? We enter here upon the contested realms of moral psychology and social ontology no less than we do of political theory narrowly interpreted.

A familiar hypothesis has it that the acquisitive impulse is a product of the conditioning of an economically materialist order, that market economies generate imperatives of ownership, consumption, and greed otherwise absent from such societies, a hypothesis supported by Rousseau's rendering of the state of nature and one frequently visible in the literature of the left. On this hypothesis one would expect that both children in Western societies and persons generally within newly emerging liberal and market orders who have yet to adopt a consumerist mentality would require indoctrination on a grand scale in order to overcome, in the first case, infantile drives and, in the second, centuries of religious and moral belief. One would expect possessive behavior to be unknown in both cases, attachment to material objects to be a foreign concept to which conditioning is met with powerful resistance, and that sharing and generosity are far more easily instilled in children than is possessiveness.

A more plausible hypothesis regards the ownership of property and the occupation of social space as contiguous with human agency itself, a hypothesis that I explore further in the course of this chapter and which is variously suggested in the political thought of Locke and G. W. F. Hegel as well as in the psychological writings of William James. The latter, for instance, speaks in *The Principles of Psychology* of materiality as being among the "constituents of the self."[4] Along with our bodily existence and family relations, James speaks of articles of clothing, the home, and other property items as forming the material or empirical aspect of the human being:

> The Empirical Self of each of us is all that he is tempted to call by the name of *me*. But it is clear that between what a man calls *me* and what he simply calls *mine* the line is difficult to draw. We feel and act about certain things that are ours very much as we feel and act about ourselves. Our fame, our children, the work of our hands, may be as dear to us as our bodies are, and arouse the same feelings and the same acts of reprisal if attacked. . . . We see then that we are dealing with a fluctuating material. The same object being sometimes treated as a part of me, at other times as simply mine, and then again as if I had nothing to do with it at all. *In its widest possible sense*, however, *a man's Self is the sum total of all that he* CAN *call his*, not only his body and his psychic powers, but his clothes and his house, his wife and children, his ancestors and friends, his reputation and works, his lands and horses, and yacht and bank-account. All these things give him the same emotions. If they wax and prosper, he feels triumphant; if they dwindle and die away, he feels cast down.[5]

On this view, the acquisitive impulse is less a product of cultural conditioning or hegemonic manipulation than it is a universal aspect of personality psychologically akin to bodily identity.[6]

The question of ownership and its relation to human agency is central to the analysis that follows; however, before turning directly to this issue, I first examine the ancient association of the sphere of private life with the domestic realm, since it is here that we find perhaps the most fundamental misunderstanding of privacy that has ever existed and which continues to inform current discussion of privacy and the public/private distinction.

DOMICILE

The case for regarding public and private as two distinct realms of social life has since ancient times been premised on a conception of the private sphere as being principally that of the household. The private realm is the domicile, an area of physical space in which marital and family relations, as well as those of master and servant, prevail over social involvements of a "public" nature. Public involvements bring to bear virtues, capacities, and identities fundamentally different from those that prevail in domestic relations. It is our identities as citizens (as ostensibly equal members of a body politic) that are brought to bear in public forms of interaction, while our private identity (as spouse, parent, etc.) is reserved for personal or private life. On the traditional conception, public and domestic relations are qualitatively distinct forms of intercourse and are governed accordingly by distinct normative principles. A moral vocabulary of care and concern that may prevail in domestic relations is not transferable to the public realm, where principles of human rights, including equality, govern the conduct of citizens and institutions alike.

A classical expression of this interpretation of the public/private distinction—or, more accurately, dichotomy—is provided in Locke's *Second Treatise of Government*, wherein Locke provides extensive discussion of the differences between political and domestic society. For Locke, a key point of the distinction lies in the equality of rights that in principle obtains in political society and the purported necessity in domestic relations of patriarchal rule. The latter point, while readily granted by Locke's seventeenth-century audience, is problematic for Locke given his explicit denial in the same text of natural hierarchies or power relations of any kind in the state of nature. How, given the absence of inequalities both in the state of nature and in political society, does the paterfamilias come to preside over the domestic realm? Locke replies that with respect to parental authority children live under the rule of father and mother by reason of the natural incapacity and dependence of the young:

> *Children*, I confess are not born in this full state of *Equality*, though they are born to it. Their Parents have a sort of Rule and Jurisdiction over them when

> they come into the world, and for some time after, but 'tis but a temporary one. The Bonds of this Subjection are like the Swadling Cloths they are wrapt up in, and supported by, in the weakness of their Infancy. Age and Reason as they grow up, loosen them till at length they quite drop off, and leave a Man at his own free Disposal.[7]

Locke emphasizes the limits of parental rule, including its limited temporal duration and the fact that such rule extends neither to the power of life and death nor even to disposal over a child's property rights.[8] Locke explicitly assumes that parents love their children and that relations between them are by nature peaceful and well ordered, assumptions that equally inform his analysis of marital relations.

What Locke terms "conjugal society" consists in both a voluntary union of man and woman and a "Right in one anothers Bodies," the chief object of which is reproduction.[9] In accounting for how it is that a woman comes willingly in domestic society under the authority of her husband, Locke proposes that husband and wife, "having different understandings, will unavoidably sometimes have different wills too; it therefore being necessary, that the last Determination, *i.e.* the Rule, should be placed somewhere, it naturally falls to the Man's share, as the abler and the stronger."[10] Locke qualifies this rather meagerly in the claims that a man may not kill his wife and that "in many cases" the latter may separate from her husband.[11] She as well retains a right over her personal property. With respect to the relation between head of household and domestic servants, an asymmetrical relation is redeemed by Locke, this time on contractual grounds—servants having sold their labor to the master as a voluntary exchange in return for wages—even as the asymmetry of the relation here again is limited, this time not by the law of nature but by the terms of a contract. Slaves, on the other hand, being captives of a just war, forfeit all rights whatever and are "by the Right of Nature subjected to the Absolute Dominion and Arbitrary Power of their Masters."[12]

Locke assumes throughout his rather unremarkable analysis of domestic life that, with the exception of the master/slave relation, such relations are (or may be) governed peacefully by the law of nature; the authority of the paterfamilias will in the usual course of things be exercised with due benevolence over wife, children, and servants. So unproblematic are such assumptions for Locke, as for the great majority of his contemporaries, that the prospect of domestic life constituting a state of war receives scarcely any comment. Throughout his analysis the thrust of Locke's argumentation is intended precisely to demonstrate that conflict may be rationally dispelled from the household, a crucial premise for the conclusions that private life is categorically distinct from public affairs and that it need not receive political regulation. Children, for instance, receive protection from the law of nature alone against the threat of abuse, protection by public institutions being both unnecessary and unjust infringements upon the private realm. For these conclusions to hold, Locke also relies on the premise that paternal authority is distinct in kind from political authority—a statement that essentially translates into the claim that the lord of the manor may not exercise the power of life and death over other occupants of the household.

Another classical account of the private sphere and its distinction from political society is provided in Aristotle's *Politics*. Following Plato, Aristotle identifies family life as the appropriate starting point of political reflection since it constitutes the most natural form of human association. The household, or *oikos*, conceived as the intersection of family and property, represents a private realm distinct in principle from the *polis*, wherein issues of state are resolved by citizens on a common basis. The principal point of the distinction between public and private turns upon the kind of power relation operative in each domain. On the metaphysical premise that every form of human association (as every human life) aims at a particular good which it seeks to realize in the general course of its existence, and on the ethical premise that the good life for man consists in the life of virtue, Aristotle argues that all authority naturally falls to that person or persons who are capable of displaying virtue in the highest degree—free adult men. The position of head of household naturally belongs to the adult male, since in him the virtues receive their highest expression—women, children, and slaves being of an ethically and metaphysically lower order. By contrast, the public realm is composed of citizens, all of whom are free adult men and, accordingly, all of whom are approximately equal with respect to virtue. With none being commissioned by nature to the position of ruler or subject, citizens properly rule by turns, each alternately serving as ruler and subject. The point to emphasize here is that power relations within the household are, for Aristotle, a natural or metaphysical given. Only in political society does the allocation of power permit controversy.

The accounts offered by Aristotle and Locke of public and private as, respectively, political and domestic society and the analyses that both provide of domestic power relations in particular are among the most orthodox such accounts within the Western tradition, and not coincidentally both are among the more frequent targets of contemporary criticism. The direction of this criticism is well known. Such accounts presuppose a host of assumptions that range from the metaphysically dubious to the naive to the manifestly false. Metaphysically, the tradition of natural law on which orthodox accounts typically rely is, in this postmodern or postfoundationalist age, a dubious starting point for political theory, one that embroils the theorist in ancient and interminable debates from which deliverance is unlikely. Still more troublesome is the evident naivete of both traditional conceptions of gender and conceptions of domestic life as being, by nature, free of antagonism, crucial premises for apolitical conceptions of the household. The following text, from *The Second Treatise*, illustrates the point in dramatic fashion:

> And though the *power of commanding and chastising* them go along with it, yet God hath woven into the Principles of Humane Nature such a tenderness for their Off-spring, that there is little fear that Parents should use their power with too much rigour; the excess is seldom on the severe side, the strong byass of Nature drawing the other way.[13]

Contemporary findings regarding child abuse rather give the lie to such sentiments, as do statistics on spousal assault, considerations that paint a less blissful picture of family life than that assumed within traditional accounts.

The political significance of this point should not be underestimated. In the face of overwhelming social-scientific evidence indicating the prevalence of physical, emotional, and sexual abuse in domestic settings, it is no longer possible to exempt such relations from political regulation, to regard the claim of private property as an excuse for violence, or to conceive of family life as by nature apolitical. Nor is it possible to conflate in simple terms the sphere of private life and the household, or property more generally. Ultimately, the direction of feminist and related criticism of traditional conceptions of private life demonstrates the imperative of severing the connection of privacy and property, whether property is understood narrowly as the home or more broadly as encompassing lands, commercial enterprises, and other economic holdings.

Any useful conception of privacy or the private sphere must render these notions in exclusively normative terms, without the physicalistic connotations handed down to us through tradition. The spatial connotation of privacy signifies a properly ethical, not physical or quasi-physical, space which protects the inviolability not only of the paterfamilias but of persons generally. As a right, the limit of privacy is marked not by material barriers but by that which constitutes the appropriate limit of human rights in general: the similar rights of other persons.

A charitable reading—if not an especially popular one—of Aristotelian, Lockean, and other orthodox depictions of the private realm is that such depictions mistake overlappings in the spheres of application of privacy and property with definitional identity. That much of what constitutes private life takes place within domestic settings accounts for the definitional conflation of privacy and household is a kind, and not wholly implausible, explanation of this traditional misunderstanding of privacy. Less charitable—and more popular—explanations are well rehearsed in feminist literature. It is likely that both explanations possess a degree of truth value, yet if feminist critiques of apolitical conceptions of domestic relations have received more attention than have rival accounts, it is hardly without just cause. So time honored and commonplace are rationalizations of domestic injustice that appeal to alleged rights of privacy or property—the often-repeated idea being that anything that transpires in the home is a matter of personal concern and that, in any event, a man is the king of his castle—that feminist correctives and efforts to highlight domestic and related power relations have served an urgent purpose. In their wake it is no longer possible to deny the political implications of much of what goes under the name of personal relationships even if, as I argue in chapter 1, a distinction of some kind between the personal and the political must be retained.

If the domestic realm is the site of mutual care and concern between intimates in private forms of association, it is also the site of power relations and injustices that clearly necessitate public remedy. No mutually exclusive disjunction exists between these two claims; however, one may wish to emphasize one or the other proposition for purposes of criticism. I return to this issue at a later point; however, we shall first need to examine the notion of property itself and the normative basis of property rights in order to clarify the appropriate relation between such rights and the right of privacy.

PROPERTY RIGHTS AND AGENCY

"For purposes of social theory," L. T. Hobhouse writes, "property is to be conceived in terms of the control of man over things."[14] This simplified definition is frequently encountered among political theorists and economists alike. Property is "anything that can be used in a market transaction"—any item, be it material or intellectual, that "has real or potential value in voluntary exchange," as Jonathon Macey concisely states.[15] Almost invariably, property is conceived in terms of rights; Robert Nozick, for instance, remarks that "the central core of the notion of a property right in X . . . is the right to determine what shall be done with X; the right to choose which of the constrained set of options concerning X shall be realized or attempted."[16] The right to property is sometimes analyzed in terms of its constituent elements or conditions, as for instance Gerald Gaus describes property rights as rights to use a given item, to exclude others from its use, to seek compensation should it be damaged by another, as well as to sell or transfer any of these rights.[17] Hobhouse identifies certain conditions that distinguish a property claim from mere possession or control of an object:

> His possession must in the first place be recognized by others, *i.e.* it must be of the nature of a right. In the second place, with regard to things of a permanent

> nature, his right must also have a certain permanence. He must be able to count on the use of the thing. His right over it, though it may be limited in time, must not be confined to the moment when he has it in his hands, but must be respected in his absence. Thirdly, his control must be exclusive. If he shares the control of the thing with others, then it is not his private property.[18]

Whether property is private, common, or joint, Hobhouse points out, it is necessarily exclusive of persons not enjoying property rights in a given object.

With respect to objects of property, land is perhaps the principal exemplar of this, along with the home and its contents, money, and private possessions such as clothing or personal effects. Material items of obvious exchange value continue to be the most commonly identified with the notion of property, even as intellectual objects such as copyrights and patents have gained an increasing presence in contemporary economies. Indeed, since the seventeenth century the modern era has witnessed a significant broadening of the concept of property to include anything whatever that can be rightfully claimed as one's own, including one's life and liberty, labor, ideas, or even the self. As James Madison noted in the eighteenth century,

> Property . . . in its particular application means "that domination which one man claims and exercises over the external things of the world, in exclusion of every other individual." In its larger and juster meaning, it embraces every thing to which a man may attach a value and have a right; and *which leaves to every one else the like advantage*. In the former sense, a man's land, or merchandise, or money is called his property. In the latter sense, a man has property in his opinions and the free communication of them. He has a property of peculiar value in his religious opinions, and in the profession and practice dictated by them. He has property very dear to him in the safety and liberty of his person. He has an equal property in the free use of his faculties and free choice of the objects on which to employ them.[19]

There is a danger involved in so broadening an ethical or political concept's signification that it no longer picks out anything that is specific or capable of being understood, as we see in counterintuitive notions of owning one's labor or oneself. What might it conceivably mean to own oneself, for instance? What clarification does it introduce to the relationship between the subject and itself—that it may transfer itself to another in an economic transaction? Is this even an interesting description of selling oneself into slavery, or is it linguistic nonsense?

For the purposes of this argument, I speak of property in the less controversial sense as anything that can be exchanged in a market transaction—whether it be material or intellectual items—and property rights as a socially and legally recognized title to control the disposition of, and to pursue profit by means of, a given item. I leave aside the ancient question whether property is or is not "natural." The metaphysical premise of this question is that existence is divided into natural and conventional (or cultural) orders, of which the latter alone, or elements thereof, is alterable and potentially dispensable, while the former is a necessary factum of existence. Much philosophical discussion of property has since ancient times been premised on the notion of a law of nature, which must be consulted for a pronouncement on property, as on a variety of issues. To this day much discussion continues to proceed on this basis, even as the dichotomy of nature and culture has long since been deconstructed and in myriad forms. Whether we may find a normative basis for the right of private ownership will no more be resolved by embedding this right within a particular metaphysical order of things than will any other question of political philosophy.

In particular, I do not approach the issue of property rights from the classical liberal standpoint of the state of nature, whether this is conceived in quasi-historical terms or in more contemporary fashion as a counterfactual thought experiment. Such an enterprise, as I have argued elsewhere,[20] assumes at once too much and too little. First, it draws upon a variety of metaphysical and epistemological premises (pertaining in particular to reason, foundationalism, and the self) that are either untenable or, at the very least, more controversial than their proponents maintain. Second, contractarian or state-of-nature theorists typically bracket many particularities that ought to be taken into account in political reasoning—such particularities as who we ourselves are as citizens and moral agents rather than as dehistoricized and instrumentally rational bargainers. The conceptual device of the state of nature, of course, has its roots in the political thought of the seventeenth and eighteenth centuries—in particular, Thomas Hobbes, John Locke, and Jean-Jacques Rousseau—and it has enjoyed something of a renaissance since the publication of John Rawls's *A Theory of Justice* in 1971. For social contract theorists of the seventeenth and eighteenth centuries, the question of property is essentially one of natural law, where the content of such law is identified by means of the faculty of reason. The law of nature, on more influential accounts, enjoins a natural right of property which is prior to civil association and in the service of which such association is formed. For Locke, for instance, it is precisely for the protection of property rights conceived in a broad sense that human beings enter into lasting forms of civil association and consent to the social contract. "The great and *chief end*," he writes, "of Mens uniting into Commonwealths, and putting themselves under Government, *is the Preservation of their Property*."[21]

This doctrine remained dominant in liberal thought of the eighteenth century and was supplemented or surpassed in the century that followed by utilitarian arguments originally proffered by David Hume and refashioned by Jeremy Bentham and other utilitarians of the nineteenth century. The natural rights doctrine was succeeded by a series of arguments for property rights which continue to carry influence to the present day, principally within liberal circles. One such argument regards property as a necessary means of preserving freedom or indeed as an aspect of freedom itself. Other arguments regard property rights as being conducive to optimal productivity and wealth creation as well as to social and economic security. A popular argument holds that persons are entitled to the fruits of their labor, while still other arguments continue to find expression.

Perhaps the most influential case for property rights, however, is the labor theory that Locke presents in *The Second Treatise*. It is here that the classical liberal case for the primacy of property receives its most important articulation. Taking the state of nature as his theoretical starting point, Locke sets out several premises for his argument, beginning with a very broad conception of property as including human beings' "Lives, Liberties and Estates, which I call by the general Name, *Property*."[22] Locke introduces the further premises that, while in their natural presocial condition, human beings are equal with respect to their natural rights, including their property rights, they are not necessarily equal in their possessions. How does it come about, then, that in the state of nature goods originally held in common come under unequal distribution, and under what conditions is the distribution just?

In addressing these questions Locke puts forth the novel idea that an individual is the natural owner of his or her person as well as of his or her labor. At once a moral and metaphysical claim, Locke holds that a human being is the rational "*Proprietor of his own Person*, and the Actions or *Labour* of it,"[23] a proposition foundational to the argument that follows. Locke has us imagine the condition of a propertyless individual in the state of nature. A solitary being, he or she must practice self-reliance to provide for the basic needs of life, including nourishment. Happening upon a plum tree, our hungry solitary takes of the fruit and eats. This acquisition of formerly common property is rightful, Locke argues, yet on what grounds? How and when does a natural resource held in common—or not held at all—become an object of private property such that its acquisition or consumption requires the consent of none? It is, Locke replies, the act of picking the plum that removes it from its natural state and transforms it into an object of private property. Given that a person has a natural right to preserve one's life and own one's labor, picking the plum creates a property right over the plum by means of mixing one's labor with it. Property, accordingly, has its origin in labor. A plot of land becomes an object of private property by the same means: by working the soil or perhaps building a fence to enclose it from the common sphere, the property right over one's labor extends over the object of labor.

Were the individual alone in the world, no principled limit would exist to the private acquisition and consumption of natural goods, yet Locke does introduce two qualifications to his notion of original acquisition. One can legitimately claim a right of property over as many goods as one wishes, provided that "there is enough, and as good left in common for others."[24] Locke introduces a further qualification, that the goods one appropriates must not be so numerous as to spoil before one can consume them. This last provision, however, is quickly disposed of with the introduction of money; as long as one may exchange goods for money—a property that does not spoil—one may acquire as many such goods as one can mix one's labor with, provided that one sells them before they spoil. This problem aside, then, we are left with the principle of justice in original acquisition as being contingent upon labor and limited by there being "enough, and as good left," for others.

Of course, Locke fully realizes that the acquisition of a property right normally does not involve taking an object out of its "natural" state but gaining it by means of voluntary transfer from a previous owner. The issue, however, is how it originally came under a private property right given the quasi-historical postulate that "in the beginning" all environmental objects were held in common. Property relations, Locke argues, including sizable disparities in wealth, can be regarded as being legitimate on the conditions of justice in original acquisition and in subsequent transfers—conditions, Locke maintains, that tend to redeem the economic conditions of seventeenth-century England. Indeed, so convinced is Locke of the merits of his case for property rights that he dismisses out of hand those who would subject this right to popular consent as "quarrelers and quibblers," whose agenda can only be to divest persons of their wealth.

At the present time defenders of property rights appeal about as infrequently to original acquisition arguments as to doctrines of natural law and natural rights. The most prevalent view among contemporary theorists is that while original acquisition arguments may carry a certain intuitive appeal (an appeal largely based on the idea that one deserves to keep the fruits of one's labor), they fail to carry any significant justificatory weight. In Locke's case, for instance, the "enough, and as good" provision is commonly found an impossible condition to realize. As Judith Jarvis Thomson writes, if "the first labor-mixer must literally leave as much and so good for others who come along later, then no one can come to own anything, for there are only finitely many things in the world so that every taking leaves less for others."[25] If every settler on the frontier must leave not only "enough" but "as good" or as much land for settlers yet to arrive on the scene, no stake whatever can be claimed. Such, it seems, is true a priori. On the other side, as David Schmidtz argues, Locke's provision not only permits acquisition but requires it, including under conditions of scarcity, for the reason that laboring upon a natural resource increases rather than decreases the supply of goods. "It is possible," he writes, "to appropriate without prejudice to future generations. Indeed, when resources are scarce, it is leaving them in the commons that would be prejudicial to future generations."[26] Goods held in common, Schmidtz argues, tend to diminish through overuse while under private ownership the individual property holder rationally consumes only as much of a resource as the conditions of its future use allow. Moreover, such labor-mixing activities as private agriculture tend to produce more such goods than does land in its original, uncultivated state, a consideration that again counts in favor of the Lockean account.

A very different argument for property rights from that of Locke and the classical liberal tradition is provided by Hegel in *Elements of the Philosophy of Right*. Hegel argues that while property is most often regarded as a means of self-preservation and freedom, it is more appropriately conceived as being constitutive of freedom itself. For Hegel, property quite literally is freedom, not in the sense that liberty or human rights in general are derivative from property rights, but that freedom of spirit or personality requires concrete embodiment for it to exist. In Hegel's words, "the person must give himself an external *sphere of freedom* in order to have being as Idea."[27] For Hegel the idealist, the individual's will belongs at the very core of his or her existence or subjectivity, and the basic movement of this is to actualize itself continually—to "make itself at home"—in the world. Personality actualizes itself in the transition, as it were, from the realm of inner subjectivity to that of external objects. It does not exist in any transcendent or disembodied form but gains existence "as Idea" in the culmination of a developmental process within ethical relations. Individual personality, or will, actualizes itself within a community of wills and in the world of external things rather than in being closed up within an inner sphere. In establishing a place for itself in social reality—a properly ethical and social undertaking—the human personality establishes itself and its freedom.

Essential to this is what Hegel describes as the placement of will in an object of the external world. It is here that property rights have their basis. "A person has the right to place his will in any thing. The thing thereby becomes *mine* and acquires my will as its substantial end (since it has no such end within itself), its determination, and its soul—the absolute *right of appropriation* which human beings have over all things."[28] Appropriation of property belongs to a process in which the will realizes itself concretely in the world and in which social reality loses its appearance as alien externality. In "[making] his will a thing or . . . [making] the thing his will," a condition of the personality actualizing itself beyond its inner, subjective life is realized.[29] One might even say that for Locke the materialist, property has its ethical basis in the combining of physical labor with an object in the world while for Hegel the idealist it is the combining of will or personality with an object that affords this basis. Like Locke, Hegel insists that the recognition of property rights is fundamental to a free political order, even as the two theorists would differ dramatically in other respects. Indeed, property is so important to the process of ethical and spiritual development that Hegel describes that it is imperative, he argues, that all persons establish themselves as property owners (a proposition that raises interesting questions regarding issues of distribution and poverty[30]).

Given the radical differences in their metaphysical and methodological premises, it is unsurprising that Locke and Hegel should hold sharply differing conceptions of politics in general, including their accounts of property rights. It is on an essentially materialist level of analysis that Locke speaks of appropriating environmental objects through labor, the paradigm instances of this being picking plums in the state of nature, tilling soil, and erecting a fence. For Locke, it is the individual alone in one's "original" presocial condition—a self fully constituted in its being prior to all social, cultural, and historical involvements—that is the methodological starting point of political reflection. Such a being comports itself on the level of biological life: it seeks nourishment and shelter, provides for its needs, and maximizes its utilities as an animal of a lower order might but for its special capacities of reason and understanding. It stands to these capacities, moreover, in a particular way: not constituted by them, the individual is instead the proprietor of its own capacities, as of its very being. The subject stands to its capacities and to itself as proprietor to property, subject to object. Social relations, for Locke, are conceived in similar proprietary terms. Public institutions are products of a social contract of proprietors in the same fashion that economic practice consists in voluntary relations of exchange between individual or corporate contractors. Social involvements in general are understood by Locke within a vocabulary of exchange relations, ownership, and utility optimization.

For Hegel, these premises are all but reversed. Moral agents are far from the ahistorical subjects spoken of by state-of-nature theorists. They are constituted only through their involvements in social reality, within ethical relations and forms of community that are anything but accidental to individual selfhood. Self and world are reciprocally constituted, as are individual selves in the general course of social life. Persons comport themselves in ethical relations not in simple maximizing terms but within processes of ethical and spiritual development. Their practices are conceived on a level not of biological or material existence but of spiritual development, a standpoint from which free agency realizes itself within the only sphere in which this is possible—that of community life. Social involvements Hegel comprehends in neither individualist nor contractual terms but in a vocabulary of community, spiritual and ethical development, and mutual recognition.

No less noteworthy, however, than the differences that fundamentally separate these two philosophers on a variety of methodological, metaphysical, and political issues is the explicit appeal both make to the notion of agency and its intimacy with proprietorship. For Locke, while particular objects of property do not enter into the moral or metaphysical constitution of the individual—subjectivity, as mentioned, being fully constituted prior to property acquisition and to social relations generally—the individual's status as proprietor is fundamental to Locke's conception of agency. One stands to the world as owner to proprietary object, consumer to resource, contractor to contractor; persons and things alike are encountered within a conceptuality of acquisition, possession, and consumption. One stands even to oneself and one's faculties, ideas, and labor as proprietor to property. Given Locke's materialist commitments, it is no surprise that his analysis of social reality and selfhood should conform to a utilitarian and quasi-biological model, just as the Hegelian analysis, in accordance with its idealist premises, conceives of agency in a spiritual dimension. Common to both accounts, however, is the intuition that property is far more than instrumentally valuable but belongs in some sense to the constitution of agency itself.

It is from the standpoint of this intuition that the right of private property is appropriately conceived. Clarifying its content, however, requires bracketing—insofar as this is possible—the metaphysical assumptions that diminish this idea's normative force. In different ways Locke and Hegel invite us to conceive of property in its ontological significance or as possessing an importance to the agent that transcends the order of instrumental value. Yet what manner of importance is this? Stripped of its metaphysical trappings, how ought we to conceive the relation of agency and proprietorship? Whatever their true relation, it is undoubtedly more subtle and complex than one of simple identity, as Locke has it, yet the Hegelian account fails to provide an altogether satisfactory understanding as well.

As I have argued elsewhere, there is an intimacy between being and acting that a philosophy of moral selfhood must endeavor to comprehend.[31] The moral self is an agent, a subject of moral action no less than a being situated within tradition, language, and culture. The conditions of an individual's realizing itself as the particular moral agent it is include a domain of voluntary action, yet action is not without conditions of its own. Action presupposes a material basis just as it requires a basis in cognition, social relations, or politics. Recall William James's aforementioned observation regarding property and the sense of self. Proprietary objects, according to James, belong to the empirical dimension of selfhood. The acquisitive impulse is not merely the offspring of an economically materialistic society but rather a universal imperative of self-actualization. If the propinquity of being and acting is fundamental to moral agency, no less so is that of being and having. As the existentialists realized, the human being is not something that merely is; it is that which becomes what it is or that actualizes itself in both a cognitive and a material aspect. As a moral agent it becomes what it is principally within the realm of practice. In making choices, fashioning plans, undertaking habitual forms of conduct, and so on, it contributes to its own constitution as a subject of moral action. For this it requires a basis in materiality. Without a basis in the material order—a category that includes our bodily existence, environmental objects, and particular items of property that we have about us—neither action nor agency itself is a possibility. L. T. Hobhouse expresses this point as follows: "Material things that a man can count upon as his own, that he can leave and return to, that he can use at his will, are . . . the basis of a purposeful life, and therefore of a rational and harmonious development of personality."[32] Objects of property, whether means of subsistence, shelter, or what have you, provide a basis of purposive action—an action that is itself the determination and expression of our being.

These three values of acting, having, and being are so intimately intermingled and fundamental to moral experience that a sizable portion of that experience may be explicitly understood in terms of their mutual relations and interpenetration. Proprietorship, for instance, is as much a basis of action as it is a condition of self-actualization or even as it is a mode of agency itself. The right to hold a given item of property is indistinguishable both in theory and in practice from the right to perform a certain range of actions with respect to it—to sell it, for example, or to modify or dispose of it. By the same token, the impulse, seemingly universal to human beings, to acquire and possess belongs not merely to the shallow pursuit of material gratification but to the existential project of becoming an agent of a particular kind.

The proximity in moral space of acting, having, and being affords a degree of illumination upon two concepts long regarded, particularly within liberal politics, as being inseparable. Property and freedom, as we have seen in the cases of Locke and Hegel, have frequently been conceived as being in some sense interdependent: either property is an essential means of establishing a free political and economic order, or it is a part of the meaning of freedom itself. Even many of liberalism's critics on the left premise their critiques precisely on a conception of freedom as being directly dependent on property—the claim being that persons are not free if they lack material means of subsistence or if disparities of wealth and poverty are pronounced. While reaching often antithetical conclusions, both schools of thought glimpse in one fashion or another the interdependence of freedom and property, the questions then being what precise form this interdependence takes and what policy implications stem from it.

Familiar liberal arguments, for instance, have spoken since the seventeenth and eighteenth centuries of the essential connection of property rights and liberty, at least in an instrumental sense. Property rights have often been regarded not only as the foundation of a free market economy but as being protective of a variety of rights not limited to the economic, from free assembly to free speech. As John Adams remarked in the eighteenth century, "Property must be secured or liberty cannot exist. The moment the idea is admitted into society that property is not as sacred as the laws of God, and that there is not a force of law and public justice to protect it, anarchy and tyranny commence."[33] Two centuries later, Friedrich A. Hayek would refine this point as follows:

> What our generation has forgotten is that the system of private property is the most important guaranty of freedom, not only for those who own property, but scarcely less for those who do not. It is only because the control of the means of production is divided among many people acting independently that nobody has complete power over us, that we as individuals can decide what to do with ourselves. If all the means of production were vested in a single hand, whether it be nominally that of "society" as a whole or that of a dictator, whoever exercises this control has complete power over us.[34]

Hayek, like many other liberals, argues that property is an indispensable means of preserving freedom and of limiting power since it is less power or "capital" itself than its concentration in few hands (particularly its monopoly in the hands of the state) that gives rise to coercion. The virtue of the free market economy, for Hayek, is that it optimizes both the creation and the dispersal of wealth, thus affording at once conditions of prosperity and freedom. Political orders that elect either not to recognize property rights or so to restrict them that they are rendered ineffectual remove an essential condition of voluntary action. Indeed, even Marx himself observes the more than accidental connection in history of liberty and property, noting that the emergence of capitalism had been indispensable to the recognition of a variety of other freedoms—even if, on his view, these other rights were likely to survive the abolition of property.

Still other theorists follow Hegel's lead in regarding property rights less as a means of realizing or protecting freedom than as belonging to the meaning of freedom itself. Paradoxically, it is often libertarians and other decidedly non-Hegelian thinkers who appropriate Hegel's point most directly. John Gray, for instance, writes that "the connection between property and the basic liberties is constitutive and not just instrumental."[35] Along the same lines,

Robert Nozick argues that the connection between property and liberty is so fundamental that states that divest persons of the former—through taxation, for example—in effect divest them of the latter:

> Seizing the results of someone's labor is equivalent to seizing hours from him and directing him to carry on various activities. If people force you to do certain work, or unrewarded work, for a certain period of time, they decide what you are to do and what purposes your work is to serve apart from your decisions. This process whereby they take this decision from you makes them a *part-owner* of you; it gives them a property right in you.[36]

Nozick and other libertarians recognize no distinction between appropriating by legal force the product of a person's actions and those actions themselves.

The libertarian view, of course, constitutes a reaction against the welfare politics of the twentieth century and what it perceives as a gradual erosion of property rights since the latter half of the nineteenth century, particularly since the New Deal era. Without doubt this general period witnessed the introduction in all liberal societies of an array of regulative measures governing the uses of property and the distribution of wealth radically unlike the laissez-faire policy of the preceding era. These measures coincided with, and were justified in part on the basis of, a recognition of the thoroughly social nature of property rights. Whereas classical liberalism had often conceived of these rights as presocial natural endowments of the individual, a less metaphysical conception of rights in general as social constructions emerged and, to many, seemed to lend credibility to the argument that if property rights—or rights generally—are contingent upon social recognition, they may be appropriately subordinated to popular conceptions of social welfare. Wishing to reject the conclusion, contemporary libertarians often reject the premise as well, arguing that protection for property rights is necessarily premised on a rehabilitation of the medieval doctrine of natural rights.[37]

Were the case for property rights to depend on such medieval metaphysical notions as natural law and natural rights, it would be in a perilous condition indeed. Fortunately, there appears to be growing recognition that while the right to private property, as with all rights, is a social artifact, it is no less deserving of protection for that reason. The idea has at long last dawned that political values need be neither "prior to society" nor carved into the fabric of heaven to warrant legal protection but may be justified in nonmetaphysical terms. These terms, I suggest, pertain to the essential interdependence of property, action, and agency and to the more than instrumental relation of property to human freedom. The rationale for property rights is in this respect no different than the rationale for human rights generally; such rights constitute political conditions for the possibility of free agency and a free and peaceful society. They are fundamental conditions of agency most directly within the field of economic practice but not only there. Human action in a broad sense requires a material basis that is relatively secure and recognized in law. It is on this basis that the right of private property depends.

MORAL SPACES

The discussion of privacy rights in chapter 1 centers on the concept of social distance and the fashion in which this is regulated by tacit imperatives or pre-understandings as well as, in the cases of personal boundaries and privacy, by personal choice. Self-realization and social peace are likewise contingent upon the free assertion of boundaries in moral space, the general function of which is to protect the inviolability of the self, particularly in those aspects of its existence that are intimate or fragile. I wish now to return to this general notion of spatiality as it functions within ethical relations. I do so on the conviction, first, that while considerations of proximity in moral space have frequently been implicit to moral and political theory throughout their history, such considerations warrant interpretive treatment more explicit than what they have hitherto received and, second, that such treatment affords a perspective from which to understand the differences and similarities of property and the private sphere.

At the most fundamental level of analysis, then, in what does the ethical significance of spatiality and associated notions of boundaries, distance, and intimacy consist such that were such values absent entirely from human intercourse, something of elemental importance would be lost? What distortion is caused by their removal from social relations, and what clue does this provide to their meaning and function within such relations? These are ethical and political questions, yet at the same time they raise issues of profound psychological, sociological, and existential importance—as commonly happens when normative "issues" are treated in a more fundamental way than in standard utilitarian, contractarian, Kantian, or other orthodox approaches.

As a case in point, let us consider the notion of trespassing as it is spoken of in both political and ethical contexts. Trespassing is a particular variety of moral offense, but what distinguishes it from other varieties? And precisely what sort of harm is this? Ordinary language speaks of trespassing in the first instance as an offense with respect to property—specifically as a harm not against property itself but against the property owner. It is a harm that concerns the disposition of that property and is committed by those who occupy another's property without the owner's consent. Yet one may also trespass against persons, at least in a metaphorical sense. One may trespass upon their personal space but also upon their time, patience, attention, or affairs. In each case, trespassing involves an overstepping or transgressing of another's rightful domain, whether the right in question be formally recognized in law or remain a matter of ordinary propriety and whether the domain in question be physical territory or personal or psychological space. While a form of harm, trespassing typically involves no terrific infliction of suffering but is instead an overstepping into a physical or psychological domain in which one does not belong. How, then, might the mere occupation of space constitute a harm? The mere crossing of a boundary poses what threat to another's well-being?

In the case of material property the answer is not far to seek. Someone intruding upon another's property—one's home, for instance—threatens one's ability to determine the trespasser's general disposition. More than this, the trespasser demonstrates a willful indifference to a boundary that another has rightfully created, displaying thereby a disposition to violate boundaries far more significant than a fence or a door. The act of trespassing upon a person, or upon one's time or patience, similarly involves an overstepping into the personal or psychological space that belongs to another and which may not be crossed without one's permission. The crime of rape may be understood as an extreme form of trespassing into a territory of the self in which one does not belong and where belonging and not belonging are defined in consensual terms. If the distortion to interpersonal relations that trespassing constitutes may be conceived as an overstepping into regions of the self or the will that belong by right to another, we may understand other spatial categories within analogous terms. A boundary is a moral barrier protective of particular regions of moral or psychological space. Intimacy is a form of relationship in which another is granted access to domains of the person that are not open for general access or display.

To speak in general terms, it would appear that the ultimate significance of spatiality as a value of personal life and interpersonal relations is to ensure a field of the will wherein the self may deliberate, choose, and act but more essentially where it may merely stand in its particularity. What boundaries—be they ethical, legal, or psychological—ultimately protect are zones of inviolability within which the self merely is, or becomes what it is, wherein no obligation exists to account for oneself in terms that others must accept, and where protection from scrutiny allows for forms of self-actualization that are not realizable in public settings. The ethical and existential project of self-fashioning, or self-refashioning, is not realized in a social vacuum but crucially involves the free negotiation of proximity with others in social space, processes of selective disclosure and withholding, approaching and withdrawing. Indeed, the human existent's characteristic mode of being or standing in the world is neither to stand still nor to stand alone but to participate in the back-and-forth movement of approaching and withdrawing, revealing and concealing, accepting and rejecting, loving and despising. We live, move, and have our being in a dialectic of solidarity and aloneness, and it belongs to the task of self-realization to negotiate this dialectic by moving about in social space on a basis of mutual freedom.

To make this abstract point concrete, let us attempt to make explicit the existential significance of human rights. Philosophers have often spoken of rights in metaphorical terms as a fence that surrounds the individual and whose function is to safeguard his or her inviolability. Rights delimit boundaries in moral space that specify both what an agent may freely do and what, with respect to others, he or she may not do. An individual right is a sphere or jurisdiction of self-chosen action, one that categorically delimits what is yours and what is mine vis-à-vis choices and conduct. Metaphorically, it may be understood as a territorial demarcation in moral space between self and others where the domain of selfhood comprises both the agent and that which belongs to it. A right shields the agent from public decisions or other "interference" with its being and in so doing is indispensable to a free life. The moral agent as rightholder may not be—indeed, is not—an asocial being in any facet of its existence, yet it is at liberty to make choices concerning itself and that which belongs to it that are authoritative. Since rights afford legal guarantees that one may choose and act within given domains, and since voluntary action is a condition of moral agency, rights in general may be conceived as conditions of individual selfhood. Spatiality, accordingly, makes possible or constitutes the ground on which individuals stand in their particularity. It affords a field of the will in much the way that Hegel speaks of property rights as actualizing freedom of the will or personality.

What light, then, does this general analysis shed on the differences and similarities of property and the private sphere? As rights, both may be understood as demarcations in social space, and in a sense that is less metaphorical than many other rights. While all rights in a sense create boundaries and zones of inviolability, property and privacy rights do so in a more direct and literal way, establishing relatively unambiguous territorial differentiations between physical, intellectual, or personal domains and the realm of public affairs. Both rights are fundamental to the free negotiation of interpersonal proximity which is an elementary and pervasive feature of ethical relations.

What has been less understood in the history of political philosophy are the differences between these two realms. While clearly overlapping in their applications, the qualitative difference between these domains concerns the type of space that is appropriate to each. The domestic realm is a location in physical space; its boundaries are physical, and the act of trespassing upon it is a matter of uninvited occupancy of territory belonging by right to another. The sphere of property more generally again is composed of physical objects and quasi-objects; it is a material space, boundaries of which are empirically demarcated. Infringing upon property rights has a correspondingly physical connotation: one trespasses upon another's land by physically standing on it; one violates another's property right in an object by stealing it, destroying it, or otherwise affecting its disposition without the owner's consent.

Privacy, on the other hand, is a region in ethical, not physical, space alone despite its ancient association with domesticity. The boundaries that it erects occur within intersubjective space and are of a decidedly nonphysical variety. Although privacy may be violated through the act of physically opening a door or a file, it is not, strictly speaking, the region behind the door or the material documents within the file that constitutes the subject's privacy but the intimate or personal nature of what is disclosed thereby. The bedroom door flung open to the indignation of the persons behind it is a privacy violation not because the private realm is constituted in whole or in part by the physical territory located between four walls but because of the intimate nature of what occasionally takes place there. Just as psychological boundaries protect the emotional inviolability of the psyche, property lines protect economic holdings from physical or economic transgression, and privacy markers protect intimacies and regions in ethical space that in being intruded upon are violated or destroyed.

A second and more subtle difference between property and privacy concerns the manner in which persons typically stand to these spheres or their characteristic mode of comportment within each. Property relations tend to fall within the province of strategic action, as proprietary objects are prized above all for their use value. To hold a property right in an object is to have a power of disposal over it or to preside over it as owner to possession. The Lockean proprietor appropriates goods in the state of nature and civil society alike in straightforward utilitarian fashion: property is a means to the ends of survival and security. Private life, on the other hand, is concerned with personal meanings, self-understandings, and interpersonal intimacies that have little to do with strategic action or cold use value. Privacy encompasses areas of human existence that resist articulation in the vocabulary of utilitarian economics—realms of sexuality, bodily existence, or creative expression to which we stand not in the capacity of lordship but in an altogether more profound way. One does not preside over this realm of existence so much as struggle continually to understand and fashion oneself within it.

Both distinctions I have just drawn, as with all distinctions that pertain to human beings, are not rigid dichotomies for which overlappings and ambiguities are unknown. As with the public/private distinction itself, the categories of property (including the home) and private life frequently overlap in their applications and shade into each other while being roughly distinguishable in abstract terms. Examples that illustrate this point are many. An object of intellectual property such as a musical recording may be of the most profound personal significance to the artist who composed and performed it even while it does not for this reason belong within the realm of the artist's private affairs; as an object of actual or potential economic exchange, it assumes a property signification that it would not have otherwise had. On the other hand, a musical recording may stand to its performer as nothing more than a commercial endeavor of no personal significance whatever. What is determinative here is not the artist's feelings toward his or her product but the status of the product as an item of exchange. The same can be said for objects more conventionally associated with property. Shareholders of a corporation, for instance, may regard their shares from the standpoint of profit potential alone without a trace of feeling for what that corporation may symbolically represent. Then again, its owner may be a Randian industrialist. The owner of a fine rococo table may regard it strictly from the point of view of its use value—what it may fetch at auction or what household objects may be indifferently tossed upon it—or, as one may hope, from the standpoint of the collector or antiquarian.

Endless examples of this kind may be offered. What they illustrate is not the nondistinction of private life and property but the relative nature of the distinction and their applicational overlappings. In light of this, it is more appropriate to understand these values as being at polar ends of a continuum, along which many gradations and subtle shades of difference are found. This is not a startling proposition given the essential complexity and multidimensionality of ethical life in general, particularly in its more fundamental and existential aspects. The importance and usefulness of many a normative distinction are not negated by what are often ineliminable complexities, even as for theoretical and practical purposes alike we endeavor to clarify the phenomena insofar as they themselves permit.

INTELLECTUAL PROPERTY RIGHTS

As if the issue before us were not complicated enough, we have witnessed in recent years increasing discussion of a species of property rights that from both philosophical and pragmatic points of view appears to problematize further the general issue of property rights, the basis of their justification, and their relation to privacy. Intellectual property interestingly differs from property in its more usual connotation, referring as it does to forms of property less tangible than land, factories, or houses, raising the question whether differences of form make a moral difference. Justifications of property rights often regard land as the exemplar of proprietary objects, with all other objects being more or less analogous to it should they qualify as property. In the case of intellectual property the analogy is not readily seen, as Hegel already remarks in *Elements of the Philosophy of Right:*

> It may be asked whether the artist, scholar, etc. is in legal possession of his art, science, ability to preach a sermon, hold a mass, etc.—that is, whether such objects are *things*. We hesitate to call such accomplishments, knowledge, abilities, etc. *things*; for on the one hand, such possessions are the object of commercial negotiations and agreements, yet on the other, they are of an inward and spiritual nature. Consequently, the understanding may find it difficult to define their legal status, for it thinks only in terms of the alternative that something is *either* a thing *or* not a thing (just as it must be *either* infinite *or* finite).[38]

The issues here are myriad; however, the question relevant to us concerns the normative justification of intellectual property rights, specifically whether they are entailed by property rights in their usual, more restrictive sense, whether their basis lies in privacy considerations, or whether they should not be treated as rights at all.

We have in the case of intellectual property an interesting test case for the argument presented earlier, one increasingly relevant to a range of economic and public policy issues. If, as I maintain, a principal point of distinction between the realms of property and privacy concerns the kind of space that each constitutes—the former having an empirical and physical connotation that is absent from the latter—intellectual property may appear not to be a form of property at all but to be closer in meaning to privacy or to constitute a separate category altogether. Another possibility is that intellectual property stands as a counterexample to the account offered earlier and thereby undermines it.

In taking up this matter it is important to clarify the meaning and object domain of what goes under the name of *intellectual property* and how this is distinguished from property as traditionally conceived. In the simplest terms intellectual property refers to the domain of human expression or ideas. It includes copyrighted material, patents, trademarks, trade secrets, and other similarly ideational matter. To be precise, it is not ideas themselves that make up this category but their tangible expressions or embodiments. Musical recordings, writings, inventions, computer software, photographs, and so on, which have their creative basis in the intangible realm of subjectivity or ideas, become proprietary objects not in their "original," ideal form but in only their concrete expressions. A scientific hypothesis, for example, is not an object of intellectual property, while its expression in written text is. Like property in its original connotation, it refers to marketable commodities, albeit ones that originate in creative thought.

One important point of distinction between these two varieties of property concerns the nonexclusive nature of intellectual proprietary objects and, related to this, the popular acceptance of intellectual property theft, which stands in marked contrast to prevailing attitudes regarding ordinary theft. Technological advances in storing, transmitting, and copying ideal objects render theft both easy and seemingly harmless with respect to their owners in a way that ordinary stealing is not. As one observer notes,

> the unauthorized taking of an intellectual object does not feel like theft. Stealing a physical object involves depriving someone of the object taken, whereas taking an intellectual object deprives the owner of neither possession nor personal use of that object—though the owner is deprived of potential profit.[39]

By virtue of what is the unauthorized copying of a musical recording, a book, or a software program an act of theft if such an act in no way deprives its owner of that object?

A second frequently encountered argument has it that insofar as the enforcement of intellectual property rights restricts the free flow of ideas, it is prima facie wrongful. Given the high value placed on freedom of thought and expression in modern culture, measures that restrict the ability of persons to acquire ideas or ideational material without violating a creator's right of personal use of the same appear to hinder the advancement of knowledge and free thought. These two arguments provide powerful challenges to intellectual property rights and have inclined some commentators to defend such rights in terms that closely resemble, if they are not identical to, privacy arguments.

Such a defense is appropriately resisted, however, in view of evident dissimilarities between that which privacy and intellectual property rights are designed to protect. As Hegel observes, it is counterintuitive to designate ideal objects as things, as would appear necessary for them to be designated as property; their nature and origin belong more to the order of mind than to that of materiality. In this respect they more closely resemble matters that fall under the privacy umbrella than they do physical property. However, as noted, it is not ideas but their tangible products or expressions that are intended by intellectual property, and it is these that such rights protect. As objects of economic exchange, they are alienated from the realm of ideas or mind that is their source and are subject to ethical and legal consideration as such. In view of their status as exchange objects rather than intimacies or personal meanings, ideational material falls outside the scope of privacy.

That they appropriately fall within the domain of property and property rights may be seen by the following arguments. First, the utilitarian argument that intellectual property rights unduly restrict the free flow of ideas or knowledge has little application to musical recordings, patents, trade secrets, trademarks, and other ideal objects that have far less to do with the spread of human knowledge than they do with the creation of wealth. Moreover, the free circulation of ideas is a cause that is ill served by the nonprotection of intellectual property, since such nonprotection removes a powerful incentive toward the creation of new ideas and expressions. For the same reason that the nonrecognition of property rights in their traditional form removes the incentive toward wealth creation that is a necessary condition of prosperity, nonrecognition of rights regarding ideal objects removes a similar incentive toward knowledge creation. That scientists, inventors, authors, or recording artists might continue to create and discover out of altruistic motives alone, without rights to retain control over or profit by their works, is an unlikely proposition.

The same consideration applies to the line of argument that since the unauthorized copying of ideal objects does not deprive a creator of the right of personal use or possession, such copying does not constitute an infringement upon property rights. The reason this indeed represents an infringement stems from a creator's or owner's loss of control over what one has created, including the freedom to seek profit by the means it provides. Whether unauthorized copying "feels like theft" is immaterial to the moral question of one's right to retain control over one's own ideas and their products.

Ultimately, however, utilitarian considerations do not suffice in accounting for the ethical basis of intellectual property rights and, in particular, fail to provide an adequate account of the harm brought about by the theft or unauthorized use of intellectual objects. As previously noted, the unauthorized copying or use of ideational material does not take away an owner's right of personal use, yet it does deprive an owner of the right to control the disposition of one's creation, including the right to exclude persons from its use in the absence of agreed upon terms of exchange and, for all practical purposes, the right to sell one's product. Like ordinary theft, the unauthorized taking of intellectual property represents an overstepping upon another's rightful sphere, a domain defined by the right to determine how one's property shall be used and by whom.

From an agency perspective the difference in form between intellectual property and property in its ordinary connotation makes no moral difference whatever. Whether its object be physical or quasi-physical, the right to private property is a right of control over that object. It is a right entailed ultimately by the normative conditions of agency realizing itself within social relations generally, including within practices of economic exchange, production, and consumption. Authors of intellectual works do not surrender rights over their works by expressing or offering them within the public domain any more than do other property owners forfeit rights over their assets by placing them within the marketplace. Both varieties of property rights involve the same intermingling of personality and object that Hegel describes, a process fundamental to the fashioning of self within ethical relations and without which such relations are neither peaceful nor free.

The question of intellectual property rights has become increasingly pressing in recent years, particularly with the advent of unauthorized "peer to peer" (or P2P) file-trading software systems which facilitate the downloading of music, movies, and software from the Internet without regard for copyright. A recent ruling of the U.S. Ninth Circuit Court of Appeals (August 2004), for example, declared that Grokster and StreamCast Networks, manufacturers of the P2P software known as Morpheus, and similar P2P systems manufacturers did not violate copyright law despite the fact that the majority of the systems' users utilize them for the express purpose of illegal downloading. The court noted that while the manufacturers of P2P software did not "seriously contest that the vast majority [of files copied and distributed by this means] are exchanged illegally in violation of copyright law," and despite the fact that such software is expressly designed for this purpose, its manufacturers were not liable.[40] The effect of pirating movies and music is most directly felt by the artists themselves, of course, who receive no royalties from such arrangements, as well as by the record and film industries that publish and distribute their work. As stated in an amici curiae brief filed with the U.S. Supreme Court in 2005 on behalf of the Recording Academy and the Recording Artists' Coalition, urging a reversal of the Ninth Circuit Court's ruling, the decision "immunizes parties that are responsible for the infringement of copyrighted works on a massive scale, and effectively holds that in the face of such copyright infringement, copyright owners have no effective recourse whatsoever against such parties." The brief continues,

> The Ninth Circuit's decision thus severely limits the practical ability of right owners . . . to enforce their rights effectively against one of the most virulent species of online infringements—those carried out using peer-to-peer networks designed to facilitate infringement. . . . This is particularly true in the context of what the Ninth Circuit called today's "quicksilver technological environment," where infringements are possible, and are occurring, on a scale across the globe that nobody could ever have imagined, only a short while ago.[41]

The court's decision was based largely upon a 1984 ruling in the "Sony Betamax" case in which Sony had successfully argued against Universal City Studios that copyright violations committed by users of its video recorders were not the responsibility of the technology's manufacturer since such products had important noninfringing uses as well. The same arguments are now cited by P2P manufacturers.

At the time of this writing (June 2005), the U.S. Supreme Court has now reversed the lower court's ruling in a somewhat surprising, and unanimous, decision. The Court held that software companies in the United States may now be held liable for copyright infringements, clearing the way for lawsuits targeting Internet piracy. Speaking for the Court, Justice David Souter remarked, "We hold that one who distributes a device with the object of promoting its use to infringe copyright, as shown by clear expression or other affirmative steps taken to foster infringement, is liable for the resulting acts of infringement by third parties."[42] It remains to be seen what impact this will have on copyright violation in the United States and globally, but perhaps there is at long last room for optimism that this particular tide may be about to turn. It remains to be seen how the issue will be viewed by similar courts and governments around the world.

For our part, the issue appears about as straightforward as it did to the Supreme Court: technology manufactured for the express purpose of copyright-infringing activity on a global scale—with, granted, a legal fig leaf of legitimate uses—is a direct violation of intellectual property rights and of the spirit of copyright law. It is, to say the least, ethically problematic when an entire generation comes to regard music, film, and so on, as being within the public domain and hence as something for which they need not pay, as is quickly becoming a reality. Nor is it solely an ethical issue; it is properly an issue of public policy and law. Unless current trends are reversed, the necessary conditions of creative expression itself—or a major portion of them—may disappear entirely.

NOTES

1. Karl Marx and Friedrich Engels, *The Communist Manifesto* (Baltimore: Penguin, 1971), 96.

2. Jean-Jacques Rousseau, *A Discourse on Political Economy*, in *The Social Contract and the Discourses*, trans. G. D. H. Cole (New York: Knopf, 1973), 151.

3. An interesting case in point is provided by the Canadian constitution of 1982, in which property rights are conspicuously absent from its Charter of Rights and Freedoms, an omission included for the purpose of removing a traditional barrier to expropriation and large-scale redistribution for public ends.

4. William James, *The Principles of Psychology*, vol. 1 (New York: Dover, 1950), 292.

5. James, *Principles of Psychology*, 291.

6. This view is similarly defended by Richard Pipes in *Property and Freedom* (New York: Knopf, 1999).

7. John Locke, *Two Treatises of Government*, ed. Peter Laslett (Cambridge: Cambridge University Press, 1988), 304.

8. "His Command over his Children is but temporary, and reaches not their Life or Property. It is but a help to the weakness and imperfections of their Nonage, a Discipline necessary to their education: And though a *Father* may dispose of his own Possessions as he pleases, when his Children are out of danger of perishing for want, yet *his power* extends not to the Lives or Goods, which either their own industry, or another's bounty has made theirs." Locke, *Two Treatises of Government*, 311.

9. Locke, *Two Treatises of Government*, 319.

10. Locke, *Two Treatises of Government*, 321.

11. Locke, *Two Treatises of Government*, 321.

12. Locke, *Two Treatises of Government*, 322–23.

13. Locke, *Two Treatises of Government*, 312.

14. L. T. Hobhouse, *Liberalism and Other Writings*, ed. James Meadowcroft (Cambridge: Cambridge University Press, 1994), 178.

15. Jonathon R. Macey, "Property Rights, Innovation, and Constitutional Structure," in *Property Rights*, eds. Ellen Frankel Paul, Fred Miller, and Jeffrey Paul (Cambridge: Cambridge University Press, 1994), 183.

16. Robert Nozick, *Anarchy, State, and Utopia* (New York: Basic, 1974), 171.

17. See Gerald F. Gaus, "Property, Rights, and Freedom," in Paul, Miller, and Paul, *Property Rights*.

18. Hobhouse, *Liberalism and Other Writings*, 178.

19. James Madison, *The Writings of James Madison*, vol. 6, ed. Gaillard Hunt (New York: G. P. Putnam's Sons, 1906), 101.

20. See Paul Fairfield, *Moral Selfhood in the Liberal Tradition: The Politics of Individuality* (Toronto: University of Toronto Press, 2000).

21. Locke, *Two Treatises of Government*, 350.

22. Locke, *Two Treatises of Government*, 350.

23. Locke, *Two Treatises of Government*, 298.

24. Locke, *Two Treatises of Government*, 288.

25. Judith Jarvis Thomson, *The Realm of Rights* (Cambridge, Mass.: Harvard University Press, 1990), 330.

26. David Schmidtz, "The Institution of Property," in Paul, Miller, and Paul, *Property Rights*, 61.

27. G. W. F. Hegel, *Elements of the Philosophy of Right*, ed. Allen W. Wood, trans. H. B. Nisbet (Cambridge: Cambridge University Press, 1991), 73.

28. Hegel, *Elements of the Philosophy*, 75.

29. Hegel, *Elements of the Philosophy*, 76.

30. Jeremy Waldron provides an interesting discussion of this point in *The Right to Private Property* (Oxford: Clarendon Press, 1988).

31. See Fairfield, *Moral Selfhood in the Liberal Tradition*.

32. Hobhouse, *Liberalism and Other Writings*, 195. Along somewhat similar lines, John Rawls writes, "The role of [property rights] is to allow a sufficient material basis for a sense of personal independence and self-respect, both of which are essential

for the development and exercise of the moral powers." Rawls, *Political Liberalism* (New York: Columbia University Press, 1993), 298.

33. John Adams, "Discourses on Davilia, a Series of Papers on Political History," in *The Works of John Adams,* vol. 6, ed. Charles Francis Adams (Boston: Little, Brown, 1851 [1790]), 280.

34. Friedrich A. Hayek, *The Road to Serfdom* (Chicago: University of Chicago Press, 1994), 115.

35. John Gray, *Liberalism* (Milton Keynes, Eng.: Open University Press, 1986), 62.

36. Nozick, *Anarchy, State, and Utopia*, 172.

37. A representative example of this is Tibor Machan, who writes, "Capitalism is the socioeconomic arrangement of human communities that aim to preserve, enhance, and protect natural rights, primarily because, proponents believe, it is only with such a system in force that it is possible for human beings to both live in dignity and fully pursue their happiness. The basis of capitalism, namely, the right to private property, serves as a policy of concrete determination and protection of every individual's realm of personal authority, sovereignty, or jurisdiction. It enables a community's membership to know and work within a framework that treats human beings as individual moral agents." Machan, *Private Rights and Public Illusions* (New Brunswick, N.J.: Transaction, 1995), 233.

38. Hegel, *Elements of the Philosophy*, 74.

39. Edwin C. Hettinger, "Justifying Intellectual Property," in *Intellectual Property: Moral, Legal, and International Dilemmas*, ed. Adam D. Moore (Lanham, Md.: Rowman & Littlefield, 1997), 20.

40. The court further noted that "approximately 90% of the content on [peer to peer] systems is copyrighted movies, software, images and music disseminated without authorization. It is estimated that 6.2 billion allegedly infringing music files are downloaded monthly." See "Brief of *Amici Curiae* International Rights Owners Supporting Petitioners," www.ifpi.org/site-content/library/grokster-international-rights owners-amicus-brief.pdf (accessed February 20, 2005).

41. "Brief of *Amici Curiae*."

42. Quoted in Krysten Crawford, "Hollywood Wins Internet Piracy Battle," www.cnnmoney.com, June 27, 2005.

Chapter Five

Revelation

The distinction between public and private has its philosophical basis in a conception of ethical relations as—or as crucially involving—a dialectic of mutuality or solidarity on one hand and individual separateness on the other. Social relations that are at once peaceful and free preserve and negotiate tensions between privacy and publicity in much the way that individual lives involve a negotiation of imperatives impelling us alternately toward and away from other persons, neither value being more essential to our humanity or happiness than the other. As much of the business of human existence involves the creative negotiation of such imperatives, many a political judgment bears on the distinction with which we are here concerned and calls for a principled and judicious negotiation between realms of action appropriate to individual judgment and to public decision. I have argued that while the distinction between public and private is ultimately more complex than political theorists have traditionally conceived of it, the distinction remains both intelligible and consequential, its abstract meaning turning upon the manner and degree to which given areas of decision making bear upon meanings and intimacies fundamental to our self-understandings as distinct persons or small groups of persons. So conceived, it is not a metaphysical or categorical polarity as political philosophers both ancient and modern have typically asserted but a rough and ready distinction between two contingent and overlapping spheres, a distinction no less important for its considerable ambiguity.

I wish in this final chapter to widen the scope of discussion from the political narrowly conceived to the broader culture for the reason that privacy issues of the kind that I have examined are not culturally isolated phenomena but may be understood in relation to wider conditions of modern culture. Debates regarding public policy, of course, invariably play out against a background of political culture as well as a larger cultural lifeworld which affects fundamentally the form, substance, and tone of such debates. In the present context questions of privacy and its infringements gain particular intelligibility in light of what I describe as a pervasive cultural imperative of disclosure or revelation of which the publicity imperative is but one political manifestation.

The impetus to disclose, to publicize, and to unmask is among the most pervasive conditions of contemporary mass culture, its manifestations assuming myriad forms both political and apolitical and at the levels of both "high" and "popular" culture. It is an imperative visible throughout a great many manifestations and phenomena that in other respects appear entirely disparate. I outline several of these in what follows for the purpose of conveying a different kind of intelligibility on policy debates that too often are conceived strictly in terms of social utility and disutility. There is, I wish to argue, more at work in these debates than superficial differences of political commitment. Undercurrents, not exclusively or even expressly political, predispose such debates in a manner of which participants very often are unaware, and it is in rendering these explicit that social criticism in this field may acquire some much needed perspective.

The interpretive standpoint from which questions of public and private may most ultimately be viewed is afforded by a dialectic more fundamental still—that between revelation and concealment. No less ancient a distinction than the one with which we have been concerned, the revelation/concealment relation is as fundamental to the issues before us as are any of the more standard premises of political philosophy, albeit a distinction that is most often neglected in this field of investigation. To say that it is a culture of exposure in which we presently live does not dramatically overstate what is observable in a wide variety of contemporary settings, the effects of which are exclusively neither felicitous nor infelicitous but which in combination can produce an erosion in the values of civil association. In the most general terms, a culture of exposure is one that characteristically prizes revelation over concealment, scrutiny over mystique, the explicit over the implicit, the literal over the figurative, the direct over the circuitous, the empirical over the aesthetic, the practical over the imaginative, and in the realm of politics the public over the private. The latter value in each of these pairings acquires dubious signification relative to its abstract antithesis. Thus, ordinary language contains innumerable positive connotations of terms such as *openness*, *disclosure*, and *candor*, whereas *reticence*, *secrecy*, and *concealment* raise suspicion. That which lurks in shadows must account for itself by coming fully into the light of day. The shadows are a natural abode for injustice, shameful and unspeakable acts, abuse, falsity, mental illness, and abnormality. That that which dwells in shadows would elect to remain there is prima facie evidence of ignorance, deviance, or impending danger. The person who "acts suspiciously" hides, conceals, and withdraws, while the virtuous and the wise bring openness, forthrightness, and enlightenment to human affairs.

Cultures, as well as persons, generally negotiate the dialectic of revelation and concealment in one fashion or another, and ours is not alone in tending to subordinate values of the latter kind, in the pairings listed here, to their logical opposites. *Revelation* and *enlightenment*, for example, are terms with rich histories in several religious traditions. Conceptions of our common existential condition as one of obfuscation, illusion, and remoteness from the divine are familiar in Eastern and Western religious thought alike, our salvation being one with enlightenment and the disclosure of being. Similar themes are common throughout the Western philosophical tradition, from its Greek inceptions to the present day. As Martin Heidegger has reminded us, to take one example, the concept of truth itself for many of the pre-Socratics was understood as *aletheia*, or unconcealment, a notion of truth both older and more original than correspondence. Truth provides a clearing such that the things themselves may be brought out of concealment and to the understanding. This conception of truth, of course, is one that Heidegger and many others in his wake have proffered as an alternative to traditional correspondence theory.

Remaining with the Greeks, Plato famously depicted the form of the good by means of the sun metaphor. The familiar allegory of the cave and the philosopher's ascent toward the sun is as apposite to our own culture as it was to Plato's. Wisdom and the good life are not attained in the shadow world below but in the full light of being. The properly human life turns away from the subaltern realm of illusion and bondage and beholds reality in its ultimate form. Happiness, virtue, and enlightenment are inseparably linked for Plato, as they would remain through the modern period.

The advent of that period, of course, found expression in the philosophy of the Enlightenment. Here the great Age of Reason displaced the medieval period—characterized as it was by its religious obfuscation, its Dark Ages, and its brutality—and prepared the way for demonstrative reasoning (or so the story has come down to us). The notion of enlightenment introduced at this time contrasted directly with the mythologization of thought from the end of the ancient period to the age of the rationalists and empiricists. Albeit a term that itself calls for interpretation, *enlightenment* recaptured and recast the very Greek idea that human happiness, peace, and virtue are founded directly upon a metaphysics and an epistemology of disclosure. The dispelling of myth, theological distortion, and unscientific prejudice was to be the route not only to knowledge but to social peace. As the scales are lifted and the eye of the mind beholds reality in its true dimension, the shadows of ignorance and oppression are dispelled for all time.

To contemporary readers there is a charming naivete to be found in much of this. Philosophers of the contemporary period are far less prone than their counterparts of the seventeenth and eighteenth centuries to regard the history of thought as one of steady progress from the Dark Ages into the light of reason. Yet the idea persists in contemporary times that the business of reflection is principally to unmask falsity or ideology so that the things themselves—perhaps even the things in themselves—might shine through. The great prophets of our age—Marx, Nietzsche, and Freud—each worked under this assumption, albeit in importantly different ways from their predecessors. For these prophets of suspicion, nothing could be more gauche than to labor under an illusion, to be naive or sanguine with respect to our fundamental assumptions. Far worse than to draw incorrect inferences is to be held fast in a condition of false consciousness, to be mired in ideology or blinded by class interests of which we are unaware. For Marx and many of those he inspired, the task of reflection or "critique" is to expose ideology, unmask hegemony, and by this means to secure emancipation. Political thought to this day often stems from this premise, even as notions of ideology, hegemony, and false consciousness have become somewhat hackneyed.

Today the stock-in-trade of many an intellectual is—in the general spirit of Marx, Nietzsche, and Freud—to unmask, demystify, demythologize, deconstruct, or otherwise expose what had been hidden from view. The intellectual's task, in this view of things, is less to understand or to see than it is to see through, to dispel every hiding place of truth. Even as "truth" and "justice" themselves fall under suspicion and appear to many of the more fashionable intellectuals to have an air of naivete about them, still it is the art of seeing through distortion and subterfuge that is the most avidly prized. If there is one failing that the intellectual of our times dreads above all, it is to be taken in, hoodwinked by ideology that we have failed to question.

Such is the intellectual orthodoxy of our times. We shall make no claim to absolute or unconditioned knowledge, have no truck with the dogmatist or charlatan, but we shall not be deceived. In one fashion or another Marxists and post-Marxists, critical theorists, postmodernists, and others each subscribe to this orthodoxy, as do even many analytic philosophers in their cautious way. One wonders in this postmodern age whether there remains any ideology to unmask, any hegemony to expose, any dominant discourse to call into question, any stone to unturn. Is there a "voice" or a "discourse" that has yet to be rehabilitated, a marginalized entity that has yet to enter and preside over the public sphere? Time and again the premise of reflection is that the more light is shone, the closer we come to the just and the true, overlooking that every light casts a shadow and that as we multiply the lights, we multiply the shadows.

This general phenomenon is equally visible in the sciences, in politics, and in public institutions. There as well the revelation imperative holds sway over a large part of intellectual culture. We have become, as Michel Foucault has well noted, a singularly confessing society, one fascinated by personal disclosure and accustomed to increasing levels of surveillance. From the penitentiary to the psychiatrist's office, it is secrecy, reticence, and withdrawal against which our efforts are increasingly directed. Noting in particular how this phenomenon manifests itself in the discourse of sexuality, Foucault remarks,

> Toward the beginning of the eighteenth century, there emerged a political, economic, and technical incitement to talk about sex. And not so much in the form of a general theory of sexuality as in the form of analysis, stocktaking, classification, and specification, of quantitative or causal studies. This need to take sex "into account," to pronounce a discourse on sex that would not derive from morality alone but from rationality as well, was sufficiently new that at first it wondered at itself and sought apologies for its own existence. How could a discourse based on reason speak of *that*?[1]

Yet speak of that it did and in tireless detail. Sexuality became a matter of public administration, legal intervention, medical and psychiatric investigation, as well as an issue of religion and morality. It became an affair of social utility and power and was compelled to speak of itself to an array of personages.

> One had to speak of [sex] as of a thing to be not simply condemned or tolerated but managed, inserted into systems of utility, regulated for the greater good of all, made to function according to an optimum. Sex was not something one simply judged; it was a thing one administered. It was in the nature of a public potential; it called for management procedures; it had to be taken charge of by analytical discourses.[2]

In time it was not sexuality alone that would fit this description but an ever-enlarging portion of the human soul. As modern medicine and the social sciences have come into prominence, more and more aspects of the self fall under the dominion of both the revelation imperative and the normalizing judgment. The mental health professions in particular obligate persons to disclose and to speak about their instinctual drives and inner conflicts without reservation. The "talking cure," a term originally assigned to psychoanalysis, currently applies no less aptly to a variety of therapeutic schools, the premise time and again being that disclosure in the form of discourse is the surest path to the fulfillment of emotional needs or—what often comes to the same thing—normalcy. It is indeed the judgment of normalcy that has become the measure of psychological well-being in its various facets. The imperative to speak, to confess, and to compare one's own being against populational norms and statistical regularities is a pervasive fact of modern culture, one supported by psychology and the social sciences, medicine, and public institutions. If social scientists themselves—wishing to maintain the appearance of value neutrality—rarely hold out statistical norms as moral standards per se, the general culture often does so on their behalf, eagerly adopting normal and deviant as scientific renderings of good and evil. As Donald Nathanson observes,

> Sophisticated parents, teachers, or therapists no longer say that a child is good or bad. But the words good and bad have been replaced by mature and immature, productive and unproductive, socially adjusted and maladjusted. And when these words are used by the teacher, the counselor, or the therapist they carry the same weight of approbation and disapprobation as the earlier good and bad.[3]

That a de facto morality is implicit to social-scientific estimations of normalcy is particularly evident from accounts of what departs from the statistically usual. While the norms themselves may not be held out as categorical imperatives, departures from them almost invariably come under suspicion and must be called to account, the standard of adjudication most often being the very norms from which they depart.

The triumph of revelation over concealment has exercised a similarly profound effect on the political cultures of many nations, though it has undoubtedly been epitomized in America. The impeachment saga of President Clinton certainly did little to cultivate respect for the privacies of intimate association. However one regards the matter from the standpoint of "family values" (i.e., ethical normalcy), the impeachment issue awarded full reign to the argument that the lives of "public figures" admit of no privacy, no space for retreat from the public gaze, and that such is the lot of elected officials. The figure who loomed largest from a cultural point of view in this national drama is undoubtedly Ken Starr, a man who effectively transcended the particularities of a legal case to assume a symbolic significance for contemporary culture. Here is an Inspector Javert for our times, symbol of relentless scrutiny, suspicion, and guardian of public order. This representative of conservative values and moral respectability stands as a symbol of a culture for which disclosure is unqualifiably good and the claim of privacy is the moral equivalent of pleading the fifth.

Bill Clinton accurately designated the modus operandi of the impeachment campaign as the "politics of personal destruction," a phrase that does more than reflect the motives of some conservative legislators: it captures the spirit of much of contemporary political culture, or at least one dimension of it. The politics of personal destruction is one side of the two-sided phenomenon that is personality politics, the method of seeking electoral support not only by means of the winning smile and the charming manner but by acts of intimate self-disclosure (and, of course, the exposure of one's rivals). The politician with the winning personality, of course, has long been favored over more guarded characters, yet what is increasingly visible on the political landscape of the present day is that it is the politicians given to personal confession, the ones who are open books, who feel our pain, who wear their hearts on their sleeves, who have unremarkable pasts and still less remarkable personal lives who stand the best chance of electoral victory. Their personal values no less than their positions on public policy must be our own; they must prize traditional marriage and the nuclear family above all else, be openly religious yet unevangelical, have no secrets beyond the trivial, and be immune in their private dealings from impropriety or, no less, the appearance of such to a scrutinizing public.

For this the politician requires the aid of the mass media, wherein the principle of absolute disclosure knows no bounds. It is in no small measure on account of journalistic practices that much of contemporary electoral politics is beholden to personality and self-disclosure. When candidates for, and holders of, public office must rely on mass media outlets to convey their message to a mass public, and when such media are driven by imperatives to entertain and stimulate as well as inform, the politics of personality is a predictable consequence. Even if politicians themselves wished for nothing but to stick to policy discussions (something that, as we all know, has never been the case), they would be prevented from doing so by journalistic practices that increasingly conflate perception and fact, investigative reporting and tabloid entertainment. Even more so than politicians, the mass media are in the perception business and are well aware of the power that they exercise not only in fashioning the public consciousness but in constructing and deconstructing public figures almost at will. Justifications for such practices are well known: the public's celebrated right to know (that is, to know most anything that it finds either interesting or amusing), the journalist's professional obligation to uncover the truth wherever it is found (not excluding truths, or possible truths, that increase market share through titillation), the self-understanding of many journalists as the social watchdogs of our time, and (when the mask comes off) the freedom of the press to report and expose as they wish. Each of these exercises in self-legitimation conceals that the business of reporting, as a commercial practice, is to increase ratings, market share, and advertising revenue and that the way this is done is by blurring divisions between fact and "perception," reporting and amusing, observation and leering. The personal lives of individuals, of course, be they "public figures" or ordinary persons, are regular casualties of such practices. As one commentator remarks,

> Full-page photo-stories of airplane crashes, microphones thrust into the most intensely personal scenes of grief, instantaneous and vacuous television commentaries on great human tragedies accompany advertisements of dancing detergent boxes. Polished announcers, in turn, function to smooth over these inappropriate dissonances. In such situations, people need protection from the casual curiosity and commentary of uninvolved others who merely want to "*look at* what is happening." It is impossible for such viewers to respond appropriately to the human drama of all the anonymous strangers portrayed in such scenes. Instead, . . . the viewer is given implicit license to dwell upon the physical aspects of the suffering and death portrayed.[4]

There is no fitting response to the suffering of strangers but a respectful silence and refusal to leer, yet it is precisely these acts that media reports of human tragedy render impossible. There is no "bearing witness" to another's suffering via television and other news media; there is only leering, the disinterested and depersonalized gaze of the spectator.

Other aspects of popular culture are no less fascinated by exposure than journalistic reports of tragedy or scandal, from the talk show craze to tell-all interviews, exposés, reality-based television, and pornography. In each case the underlying principles are analogous, to say the least: to inform/entertain through exposure, particularly representations of what is personal, intimate, or fragile. The talk show phenomenon, for instance—ushered into existence by journalism, the mental health professions, and the entertainment industry—provides a regular succession of individuals anxious to reveal all in order to capture the public spotlight for the briefest of moments. What is noteworthy about this phenomenon from a sociological point of view, if one may call it that, is less the succession of characters onstage—from ostensible beneficiaries of the mental health professions to representatives of alternative lifestyles—than the audience. They are us, the designated representatives of normalcy and guardians of respectability. Their function is to assess and judge, often to leer and jeer, in light of social norms, and a more unforgiving audience has never existed.

If Foucault is correct in his observation that during the eighteenth century sexuality became a very public—scientific and political—matter, it has since become a still more public affair, albeit in a sense different than what Foucault describes. Hardly a sacred mystery, its representation is as ubiquitous a product as any in the marketplace of popular culture. Pornography merely carries this to its logical conclusion, exposure being its only absolute, while more reputable discussion of sexuality continues to speak of it as a utilitarian matter for which discourse and the judgment of normalcy provide the solution. Without doubt there is much in this, as with the very notion of disclosure itself, that is unobjectionable in itself. Sexuality ought no more to be a taboo subject than any other, yet one might hope for an intermediate ground between sex as mystery and sex as product.

More generally, there is much that is legitimate in the various manifestations of the revelation imperative that I have noted, and it is not my intention to argue that concealment would properly replace or outweigh disclosure. There is much truth in the hypothesis that injustice not only habitually dwells in secrecy but requires it as a condition of possibility. Political corruption, for instance, resists exposure to the light of day as its nemesis, as does domestic violence, abuse, and numerous other forms of injustice. In each instance shedding light upon the problem is indispensable both in understanding its nature and in cultivating general awareness of it, measures without which it would not be remedied. Attitudes of intolerance and bigotry can be remarkably intractable until they are brought to public attention and seen for what they are. Much of social criticism, as of interpretation generally, involves disclosing what had been hidden from view, even if the practice of criticism involves more than unmasking hegemony or ideology. Sound phenomenology as well involves an unconcealing (as Heidegger would say) of given phenomena or a bringing into the open of the things themselves without the obfuscation that prior theoretical commitments bring.

A particular example of the revelation imperative that is noteworthy for both its positive and its negative aspect is biography. What, one might ask, is the source of the biographical imperative? What impulse or passion transforms admiration of an individual's work—be it a work of art, a political career, or what have you—into a need to know about the personal history and intimacies of one's life? To be sure, one would not wish to cast aspersions on the biographical genre per se. Whatever its source, the need to feel a personal connection—real or imagined—with persons in the public eye whom we admire is timeless. We wish to see in outward form a representation of what is best within us or what we aspire to become, as well as depictions of human depravity. Each is a representation of our own potential being and as such is an object of personal fascination. Yet there is something else that is at work in the biographical imperative—a fascination with exposure for its own sake, with the confession of secrets or indiscretions that the subject of the biography would not wish for public display but which entertain an audience or provide reassurance that an admired figure is not as admirable as he or she appears. Skilled biographers do not reveal indiscriminately every scrap of information that they uncover about their subject but in their own manner must negotiate the distinction between disclosure and reticence, revealing only that which is relevant to the character of the subject and to the unfolding of the narrative.

What these disparate cases illustrate is that the relation between disclosure and concealment, as with public and private, is not the hierarchical one for which it is often mistaken but a subtle and dialectical relation between values equal in importance. While few today would plead the case of concealment, secrecy, or reticence, the neglect of these values eliminates an important break upon a culture of ubiquitous exposure and surveillance. The price such a culture pays belongs more to the order of the intangible than to the tangible—tangible in the sense of concrete social utilities and disutilities. Such a culture overlooks that while it is often the nature of injustice, falsity, and ignorance to dwell in shadows, there is something else that dwells there as well. Private reflection, inwardness, creativity, self-knowledge, dignity, significance, and the depths of life typically gravitate away from publicity and toward a condition of detachment, stillness, and concealment. While neither asocial nor antisocial phenomena, each of these is governed by an imperative of retreat—usually of temporary retreat—from everyday sociability so that conditions more fundamental or profound may be realized. Human dignity, for instance, is appropriately understood as being removed from the vicissitudes of the democratic will, quite unlike many other political values prevalent in democratic societies. Creativity and private reflection involve a similar retreat from the public realm so that an authentic voice might emerge from the noise of social life. Spiritual traditions often have it that the sacred and the divine reside at some remove from the public and the empirical, in hidden recesses of the spirit or a realm transcending the empirical and the everyday. The sacred object is inaccessible to the masses and to prying eyes that would vulgarize or violate the object by tearing it out of its remoteness and exposing it to the full light of day. The sacred is violated precisely in being uncovered in a fashion that debases it, in having every veil lifted for the amusement of onlookers.

There is a certain shallowness that reigns when a culture renounces the values to which I have alluded, an adolescent fascination with outward appearances, surfaces, and stimulation at the expense of more ultimate things. Reduction to the explicit and the public removes much of what lends profundity and significance to our existence, even as it furthers many utilitarian ends. Max Scheler has observed that

> our psychic life seems to have profound roots which function only in the shade, and a sphere of awareness and clarity in which elements are clearly separated one from the other. Clarity alone and concealment alone are equally prejudicial to the soul and its development.[5]

Privacy's function, as with concealment more generally, is to render inviolable the dimension of life that in being exposed is violated or destroyed. It is to preserve the tension of revelation and concealment that is essential both to individual well-being and to a free social order. Its decline leads directly to a vacuity and cheapening of social life which we would appear to be witnessing at present.

Underlying the revelation imperative is an imperative more fundamental still, manifestations of which we catch regular glimpses. This is the normalcy imperative or the sense, seemingly ubiquitous in modern culture, that every aspect of our existence—from private attitudes and beliefs to public acts, relationships, sexuality, and general lifestyle—must remain firmly in step with the norms of our time and place. If the exposed object is brought before the public gaze and called to account, as it so frequently is, such accounts almost invariably appeal to behavioral and psychological regularities as standards of legitimacy, quite irrespective of what the object under scrutiny is. Consider, as a case in point, the mental health professions and the profound influence that they carry at the present time. The criterion of normalcy is and has long been the sine qua non of mental health in various schools of psychotherapy. Persons whose mental suffering is acute but within parameters of normalcy have little to profit from the services of the psychologist or psychiatrist. More remarkable is the large number of such patients, and of persons generally, who register the judgment of normalcy as the modern equivalent of salvation. No matter the nature or extent of our unhappiness—a familiar premise has it—if it accords with the unhappiness of others identically situated, all is as it ought to be.

There is a broad tendency in modern culture to bring ever-increasing portions of our personal and collective existence before the public gaze, a tendency commonly touted as a step forward for social justice, democratization, critical consciousness, and other ends that are widely and rightly prized. There is considerable truth in this supposition as well, but there is no less truth in the claim that the public gaze is inherently normalizing and in a manner that is not altogether edifying. When most anything or anyone is brought before the public gaze, a tendency toward not only critical consciousness but self-consciousness and self-legitimation in their baser forms is often manifest. What is open to public scrutiny quite naturally seeks to eliminate impropriety or the appearance of this from common view, but so too, and equally commonly, does it eliminate differences for which it is sure to be called to account. What is anomalous regularly calls for explanation and legitimation, and for a legitimation that is articulated specifically in terms acceptable to the general public. Individual variance is compelled to plead its case before the tribunal of popular opinion and must be ever vigilant for when its appointed time comes. In a culture of exposure everyone must be prepared to take a turn in the public spotlight, to reveal all, and to submit to the judgment of normalcy. Should participants wish to redeem themselves by a different standard, they face a formidable challenge. A general atmosphere of suspicion compounds this challenge, accustomed as modern consciousness has become to the perception of corruption and the sense that everyone is a wolf in sheep's clothing. In a time when every intellectual aspires to be a Marx or a Nietzsche, and every journalist a Woodward or a Bernstein, one had best be prepared for the full public disclosure that, like the judgment of the Creator, could come at any time.

By all accounts, contemporary culture embodies an advanced state of individualism and is rapidly becoming one that is more respectful of difference and plurality than at any previous time in history. While there is a sense in which this is self-evidently true, it remains that the individualism of our times is frequently more apparent than real. If self-realization is among the principal watchwords of our times, it is often a counterfeit variety, qualified by ubiquitous imperatives of disclosure and normalcy more akin to social conformism than to authentic individualism. The prevalence of the normalizing judgment often renders conformity self-imposed, a survival strategy in a culture that does not condemn difference so much as call it to account, interrogate it, and compel it to confess its nature. Even as the modern subject professes individualism as a normative ideal, its manner of standing out from the mass must be acceptable to the mass, and it must practice a rigorous self-scrutiny to ensure that such standing out does not stray into deviance.

A culture of surveillance and exposure gives rise to self-scrutiny—the internalized counterpart, as it were, of public scrutiny—in both its nobler and baser forms. Students of philosophy are well aware of the virtue of self-knowledge and the perils of the unexamined life, but what becomes increasingly visible in modern culture is self-scrutiny in its excessive and neurotic forms. The anticipation of exposure compels the modern subject less to know itself in the Greek sense, or toward introspection or critical self-reflection in their modern connotations, than to scrutinize its interiors for irregularities of the soul, abnormalities of affect or behavior that could invite public censure. Christians have long been familiar with this form of self-consciousness, habituated as they have been for centuries to interrogating the self for traces of ungodliness, with the prospect of judgment hanging omnipresent about one. Now that the gods have departed, it is the public gaze that is watching or a configuration of therapists, educators, social workers, journalists, medical doctors, and public institutions that compel the subject to confess its nature and submit to the judgment of normalcy.

Modern culture makes it difficult enough for many to gain or hold on to a sense of private identity when the public gaze is not trained upon one. The everyday act of going to work for many profoundly threatens the private sense of who one is, it being no simple task to reconcile this sense with one's function in the socioeconomic machinery of mass society, with others' perceptions of oneself or other environmental conditions. When identity is intimately tied to functionality and the reality of modern economies is that all are replaceable, the sense of self is contingent indeed. The matter is exacerbated when conditions of hypervisibility exert further pressures toward sameness of being. Hypervisibility leads by a straight line to forms of self-scrutiny explicitly oriented toward social conformity while undermining visibility in its more genuine forms. Visibility as the person one is, or whom one takes oneself to be, is negated under conditions of hypervisibility and replaced with a form of anxiety related, but not identical, to shame. If shame arises from the sense that one has failed to uphold a standard or conception of the person one is—a tension, as Freud would say, between ego and ego ideal—it is less anxiety in this form that comes to the fore than an anxiety rooted in others' estimations. It is a self-consciousness in the form of constant vigilance to avoid debasement not in one's own eyes but in the eyes of an anonymous other. Hypervisibility breeds an adolescent hyperconsciousness of self very different from mature self-reflection, and it is precisely this phenomenon that has become increasingly visible in contemporary culture.

If the values of exposure and publicity have gained primacy in modern times over their abstract antitheses—their virtues celebrated in innumerable forms and their political entailments profoundly apparent in contemporary public policy—renewed attention to both the limits of publicity and the role that privacy and its associated values play redresses an important imbalance in modern political thought. For the values of private life to reassert themselves, an understanding of privacy as not only an ethical and political principle but an aspect of a wider cultural phenomenon is needed, and it is with this aim in view that the preceding reflections are offered. So long as the case for privacy rights is articulated solely in the language of social utility, it will fail to comprehend the significance and normative import of the rights it would defend. The significance, scope, and limits of the private realm are appropriately conceived in terms of areas of decision making that bear upon personal meanings, self-understandings, and intimacies that rightfully belong to persons as such if they are to exist at all.

NOTES

1. Michel Foucault, *The History of Sexuality*, vol. 1, *An Introduction*, trans. Robert Hurley (New York: Vintage, 1990), 23–24.
2. Foucault, *History of Sexuality*, 24.
3. Donald Nathanson, *Shame and Pride: Affect, Sex, and the Birth of the Self* (New York: Norton, 1992), 18.
4. Carl Schneider, *Shame, Exposure, and Privacy* (Boston: Beacon, 1977), 77.
5. Max Scheler, *La Pudeur*, trans. M. Dupuy (Paris: Aubier, 1952), 147.

Index

About the Author

Paul Fairfield teaches philosophy at Queen's University in Kingston, Ontario, and is the editor of *Symposium: Canadian Journal of Continental Philosophy*. He is the author of several books on political theory and hermeneutics, including *The Ways of Power*, *Theorizing Praxis*, and *Moral Selfhood in the Liberal Tradition*. He is also co-president of the Canadian Society for Continental Philosophy.